Acts of Knowledge

Acts of Knowledge

Pope's Later Poems

Fredric V. Bogel

Lewisburg
Bucknell University Press

London and Toronto: Associated University Presses

© 1981 by Associated University Presses, Inc.

Associated University Presses, Inc.
4 Cornwall Drive
East Brunswick, New Jersey 08816

Associated University Presses
69 Fleet Street
London EC4Y 1EU, England

Associated University Presses
Toronto M5E 1A7, Canada

Library of Congress Cataloging in Publication Data

Bogel, Fredric V   1943-
    Acts of Knowledge.

        Includes index.
        1. Pope, Alexander, 1688-1744 — Criticism and interpretation.
I. Title.
PR3634.B57   821'.5   78-75194
ISBN 0-8387-2380-2

Printed in the United States of America

*For my mother
and in memory of my father*

Contents

Preface

This is a study of structure and meaning in the later poems
of Alexander Pope; more specifically, it is about the way in
which structure and meaning articulate the central theme of
knowledge in that poetry. The study began, in one sense,
many years ago when Frank Brady taught me most of what I
know about eighteenth-century literature and critical theory;
I have continued to be sustained by his friendship and
criticism. More recently, Martin Price read and criticized —
wittily, mercilessly, and thoughtfully — an earlier version of
this book. His writing on the eighteenth century has served
throughout as an exhilarating, if impossible, standard.
Maynard Mack's criticism of a draft of Chapter 2 proved
extremely helpful; he also kindly provided me with copies
of several important manuscripts of Pope's poems.

For their criticism of earlier versions of several chapters,
and for much head-clearing discussion of critical problems, I
am grateful to William C. Dowling, John M. Fyler, H. M.
Leicester, Jr., Ronald R. Macdonald, and Michael O'Loughlin.
To my wife, Lynda, who gave this book a careful critical
reading at several stages of its composition, I owe most of
whatever readability it possesses, and much more that I
cannot begin to describe.

Finally, I owe a longstanding debt to the critical theory,
both published and declaimed, of the late William K.
Wimsatt.

I am also grateful to Connecticut College, and to the
former chairman of its English Department, George J.
Willauer, Jr., for a leave of absence during which the book
received its last revisions; to Connecticut College for a

generous typing grant; and to Patricia K. Minucci for her accurate and rapid typing.

Fredric V. Bogel
Connecticut College

Acts of Knowledge

1 The Poet and the World

i. The Poet and the World

> In a word, the world and I agree as ill, as my
> soul and body, my appetites and constitution,
> my books and business.
>   — Pope to Caryll, ?December 1715[1]

POPE'S relationship to the world, uneasy in the winter of
1715, was not destined to mellow with the passage of time.
The events of the next dozen years — the darkening of the
political scene with the rise of Walpole; the bursting of the
South Sea Bubble; and the attacks on his poetry, morals, and
person — could hardly be expected to endear the poet to
that complex fabric of show and corruption that he called
"the world." Nor was he likely to be mollified by the
increasingly frequent and severe pains of his own "little,
tender, and crazy Carcase," as his friend the dramatist
Wycherley called it.[2] In 1715, this "gayest Valetudinaire,/Most
thinking Rake alive," could still bid a jaunty farewell to
London, the "Dear, damn'd, distracting Town" that served
as his principal symbol of "the world," and that had received
the first volume of his *Iliad* with so much acclaim.[3] But to the
scarred poet of forty years in 1728, it must have seemed as
though "*Albion's* Golden Days," hopefully prophesied in
Windsor Forest, were to have their being exclusively in that
poem. For within a few days of Pope's fortieth birthday there
triumphantly appeared the first version of a new myth of
Albion, a new vision of "the world": *The Dunciad.* The
spiritual direction of England, the tendency of history, was

13

now toward Albion's Leaden Days and the triumph of chaos, "the Accomplishment whereof," it was prophesied, "will, in all probability, hereafter be the Theme of many other and greater Dunciads."[4]

Pope's complex connections with the world, his attraction or indignation or disillusionment, are not merely biographical data but poetic subjects, and remarkably persistent subjects. No matter how unworthy the world becomes, and no matter how weary the poet grows of its claims on his life, he continues to take detailed notice of it in his poetry. This mixture of detachment and involvement is, of course, a necessary condition of satire. However corrupt the world may seem to him, the satirist always joins battle with it rather than retreat to a counterkingdom of his own creation. But Pope's ambivalence toward the world is more than a satiric strategy; it is the expression of powerful and conflicting impulses. Withdrawal and isolation are at times very tempting to him, but the impulse toward a nonantagonistic relation with society, a communal identity, is equally strong. For while he is acutely aware of the imperfections of the world, he is also aware of his inexorable ties to it: "Well then, since with the world we stand or fall,/Come take it as we find it, Gold and all."[5] If Pope's satire is an expression of that "warfare upon earth" which constitutes the life of a wit, it is also, in Emily Dickinson's phrase, his "letter to the world," and the evidence of the poetry is that the poet and the world, though they may have agreed no better than his soul and body, could be separated with only slightly less risk.[6]

Such ambivalence is hardly unique to Pope. "He passed through common life," Johnson reminds us, "sometimes vexed and sometimes pleased, with the natural emotions of common men."[7] Critics since Johnson, moreover, have described with great subtlety and care the precise nature of Pope's vexations and pleasures, the nature and basis of his judgments of the world. But while modern criticism has refined Johnson's terms, disclosing the complexity of Pope's moral vision and the rhetorical mastery that articulates it, the terms themselves have persisted. Few, today, speak of Pope as "vexed" or "pleased," but fewer still grant to other dimensions of Pope's poetry the seriousness they grant to the moral dimension. At least some of the reasons for this state of affairs are relatively clear. For one thing, Pope is undeniably a moral poet, and he became increasingly so in the course of his career. He is concerned with the world of human conduct and human truths: what men do, what they believe, what they think and feel. For another, no poetic concern could have served so well to establish Pope's essential seriousness against the now outmoded charges of shallow optimism, or mere decorative elegance, or personal spite. The image of Pope as a serious and difficult moral poet was not only accurate, it was useful as well.

What this modern critical emphasis has kept us from seeing, however, is that Pope is as much concerned with the discovery of values as with values themselves, as much concerned with the problem of knowing the world rightly as with the need to value it rightly, and thus as much a poet of knowledge as a poet of morality. To recognize that Pope is a poet profoundly concerned with problems of knowledge can, first of all, help us to understand the structure of his later poetry and thus to counter the "stubborn misapprehension," as Maynard Mack puts it, "that his satires, epistles, and other poems of the sort lack unity — as they do in fact lack the unity of the reflective and dramatic lyric, the only sorts of poem for which we have as yet an adequate critical terminology."[8] For while this misapprehension has been out of fashion in recent years, it has been countered not so much by demonstrations of the structure of Pope's later poems as by a kind of pious assumption that they do, indeed, have a structure.

Further, to see that Pope's is a poetry of knowledge, and that his treatment of knowledge is as much a structural as a thematic element in his works, is also to see new principles of unity in his later poetry taken as a whole: *An Essay on Man,* the *Epistles to Several Persons, An Epistle to Dr. Arbuthnot,* the *Imitations of Horace,* and *The Dunciad.* These poems all participate in a moral attitude we have come to recognize as Pope's, but they also play variations, albeit subtle ones, on a very few patterns of poetic structure. These patterns are perhaps best understood as the poetic analogues of primary acts of knowledge in which the poet tries to discover not simply the worth but the nature of the world around him.

Pope, of course, believes in an objective world, a substantial reality external to the mind. What particularly fascinates him, however, is the variety of ways in which men cut themselves off from significant knowledge of reality, living instead in a realm of shadows, distortions, barren schemes and proud systems. At times, the poet himself suffers such confusion, but he is soon aware of doing so. And he is aware, moreover, of the degree to which individual consciousness inevitably shapes external reality:

> All Manners take a tincture from our own,
> Or come discolour'd thro' our Passions shown.
> Or Fancy's beam enlarges, multiplies,
> Contracts, inverts, and gives ten thousand dyes.
> (*To Cobham*, 25-28)

Pope's poetry thus does not give us merely an objective picture of the world, but rather communicates the varying size, shape, texture, and density of this world as it is perceived and expressed by a poetic speaker *striving* for objective knowledge. Language and structure are poetic forms of the very way in which the individual consciousness of that speaker apprehends — and thus interprets — the world.

The recognition that human knowledge is not "One clear, unchang'd, and Universal Light" need not, then, result in despair or sheer relativism. This recognition may, in fact, foster a concern with the nature of knowledge itself, a concern that is a characteristic though much underrated feature of both Pope's poetry and the literature of his greatest contemporaries. Augustan satire, as Hugh Kenner remarks in another context, "traffics in epistemologies."[9] In the fifteen remarkable years that begin with *The Dunciad* of 1728 and culminate in *The Dunciad* of 1743, one of Pope's major themes is human knowledge. This is not knowledge treated as a specialized study, the object of espistemological investigation, but knowledge viewed as a form of life, a human activity as much cognitive as evaluative: the human interpretation of human experience. Such knowledge is often the explicit subject of Pope's poetry, but even when it is not, his poems are best understood as structures of knowledge and acts of self-definition, and the poet as a man striving to know the world and himself.

ii. Modes of Knowledge

Broadly speaking, Pope's later poetry is a continuing dialogue between two modes of knowledge, schematic and substantial, and between the two kinds of world and knower that each mode implies. Schematic knowledge sees the world as a pattern or scheme, a play of clearly defined forces and principles. It abstracts clarity from muddle and contingency, and reduces the complex and opaque to the simple and lucid. In thus subduing the otherness of the world to the demands of the mind, however, schematic knowledge frequently deprives the world of its substantiality, its organic subtleties and mystery. The chief characteristic of the world of the schematic knower is, precisely, that it is known, and "Nature well known, no prodigies remain,/Comets are regular, and Wharton plain" *(To Cobham,* 208-9).

Schematic knowledge may be seen as a form of system-building or mythmaking, in which the mind and its creations exist prior to the experience they shape: "The *Poem*," as the publisher's letter to the reader says of *The Dunciad*, "*was not made for these Authors, but these Authors for the Poem.*" Or it may be seen as an abstraction or selection from experience: "Alike in nothing but one Lust of Gold,/Just half the land would buy, and half be sold" (*Epistle I.i.* 124-25). In each case, a simple scheme or pattern is preferred to the complex reality of things, whether that scheme originates in the mind prior to the act of knowledge or inheres in the object and is abstracted from it. Schematic knowledge, in Pope's poetry, is more often satiric than not, portraying a uniformly repugnant or demonic world from which the poet strives to separate himself; but there is no necessary connection between the schematic and the satiric. Schematic knowledge may also take a simplistic theodicean or Utopian form, interpreting the world so as to refashion it into a representation of the knower's desires (or those desires may be perfectly accommodated to the condition of the world). In either case, the satiric or the theodicean, the knower is disastrously alienated from the world, for each form of schematic knowledge constructs its characteristic myth and substitutes it for objective reality.

Substantial knowledge is not a simple opposite of schematic knowledge; such an opposite would be a kind of mad, radical empiricism, always observing and noting but never generalizing or formulating. Rather, substantial knowledge strives to wed the intelligibility of scheme to the dense and opaque contingency of phenomena, thereby respecting both the knower and the known, the mind's demand for order and the world's stubborn integrity. The world of substantial knowledge is "A mighty maze! but not without a plan," sufficiently lucid to be comprehended yet substantial enough to be dwelt in. Although it rejects the proud certainty of schemes and systems, substantial knowledge may nevertheless make use of the schemes and systems themselves, resisting and qualifying them with the saving humility of the provisional, the tentative. This knowledge is not merely passive before phenomena, but it has the strength to refuse inappropriate certainty. It finds its truth in a delicate combination of involvement and detachment, and it prizes the difficult inclusiveness of the double vision over the ruthless orderliness of schematic singleness. Because it is characterized by dual loyalties, substantial knowledge is frequently self-aware and ironic.[10] It is the kind of knowledge most valued by Pope, because it is most appropriate to the curious doubleness of man: the doubleness of his own nature, and of his relationship to a world in which he must live but cannot be fully at home.

At its hypothetical extreme, the satiric form of schematic knowledge has no literary expression at all; it trembles in the silence of total alienation, total outrage at all that exists. From there it moves to a Thersites-like railing ("Whatever is, is wrong") and finds its characteristic literary form in apocalyptic or visionary satire, which depicts the world as utterly lucid and uniformly demonic:

> In Soldier, Churchman, Patriot, Man in Pow'r,
> 'Tis Av'rice all, Ambition is no more!
> See, all our Nobles begging to be Slaves!
> See, all our Fools aspiring to be Knaves!
> The Wit of Cheats, the Courage of a Whore,
> Are what ten thousand envy and adore.
> All, all look up, with reverential Awe,
> On Crimes that scape, or triumph o'er the Law:
> While Truth, Worth, Wisdom, daily they decry—
> "Nothing is Sacred now but Villany."
> *(Epilogue to the Satires,* I.161-70)

As these lines suggest, apocalyptic satire tends naturally toward the tragic since it emphasizes the alienation of the One Just Man (here, the satirist) from a world whose corruption he can neither overlook nor tolerate. At the opposite extreme, the Utopian and accommodating form of schematic knowledge also abides in silence, expressing itself instead in the mindless glow of total well-being, placid and gratified immersion in all that exists. From there it moves toward various forms of naive theodicy ("Whatever is, is wonderful"), toward celebration, and — a more personal version of these — toward apology. It tends naturally toward the comic since it emphasizes the union of the knower with the world that he knows.

Pope displays something of both tendencies, the satiric and the Utopian or theodicean, but the thrust of each toward totality, cosmic vision, is qualified by a refusal to subordinate the stubbornly resistant particular to the sweeping generality of scheme. Since Pope's satires almost always include accounts of certain virtuous individuals, they avoid being "gen'ral, unconfin'd."[11] Similarly, his theodicean strain demonstrates meaningfulness rather than mere hidden pattern. It does not strip away the everyday world to disclose order beneath it, but tries instead to reveal the order that governs the everyday world, the pattern that informs and fuses with it. The result is an effort to redeem rather than replace that everyday world. Nor are the satiric and theodicean strains always strictly separated. Characteristically, each corrects the other, resisting its tendency toward total vision (far more often satiric than theodicean), recalling it to the actual complexity of the actual world. As we might expect, comedy and tragedy also tend to coexist, tempering each other's excesses and keeping alive that persistently double relation of the poet to his world and to himself.

iii. The Poem As Process

Schematic and substantial knowledge are best seen as two relatively fixed states between which the poet's consciousness moves, but it is the movement itself that constitutes the chief drama of his later poetry. The satires and epistles of the 1730s are tentative and exploratory poems, fraught with accents of inquiry and self-examination in a way that poems like *Absalom and Achitophel* or *The Dunciad* are not. In Dryden's account of rebellion and order as in Pope's epic of Dulness, the poet's role is largely defined by the narrative, the course of events that — whatever else he may do — it is his business to relate. In the poems of the 1730s, however, Pope's role is less that of narrator than of correspondent, conversationalist, or self-examiner, and his characteristic activity is less the description of certain anterior events and characters from a given point of view than the development, the working out, of a point of view or attitude. The attitude, and the labor of achieving it, are often the real subjects of the poetry. This is not to suggest that such poetry is less "serious" than more overtly grand forms. Conversational ease and an exploratory and apparently digressive structure can not only coexist with genuine depth and complexity but constitute their very form. The reader of Pope's later satires and epistles must be especially careful to avoid the mistaken notion that, as Maynard Mack puts it, "a little man who could veer so briskly, nimbly, even jocularly (and with such wit and polish!) from grave to gay and lively to severe could not possibly have understood, much less meant, those compelling insights on which the poetry opens if one takes it seriously."[12]

To give such prominence to the movement of the speaker's consciousness is to take the unfolding of that consciousness as the defining structure or plot of the poetry. "When a critic deals with a work of literature," Northrop Frye has said, "the most natural thing for him to do is to freeze it, to ignore its movement in time."[13] It is usual for the critic to do so, and in part inescapable, but it is nevertheless profoundly unnatural. Although the critic necessarily "freezes" literary movement in order to describe certain aspects of it, he must also remember that he, and not the poet, has done so, and that literature presents, in Alvin Kernan's words, "not completed man but man in action seeking form."[14] In Pope's case, that action is the poet's quest for genuine knowledge and a genuine self. This search is not a simple linear process, for these are not simple goals, and Pope is well aware that correct distinctions are hard to make:

> At last agreed, together out they fly,
> Inseparable now, the Truth and Lye;
> The strict Companions are forever join'd,
> And this or that unmix'd, no Mortal e'er shall find.
>   *(The Temple of Fame,* 493-96)

The poet's movement toward the goals of his quest is complicated and deepened by his respect for the difficulties, the uncertainties, the complexity and wholeness of the experience in which he participates.

Plot and poet, moreover, are ultimately indissoluble, the convex and concave of a single curve; for the other side of that movement which constitutes plot is the act of self-definition that it inescapably includes. This is true to a degree of all first-person literature, but it has special relevance to Pope, both as an individual poet, engaged upon a quest for knowledge that is also a quest for identity, and as a writer of the eighteenth century, that period in which, as Ernst Cassirer observes, "thought cannot turn toward the world of external objects without at the same time reverting to itself; in the same act it attempts to ascertain the truth of nature and its own truth."[15] In the *Epistles to Several Persons,* and even more in the *Imitations of Horace,* problems of the world and problems of the self are inseparable. The act of interpreting the character of others alters the interpreter; perceptions of moral enslavement in the world throw the poet's mind back on his own enslavement, emotional or epistemological. In satirizing that world, therefore, Pope conducts a thoroughgoing, though often indirect, critique of his own satiric assumptions and his own poetic identity. To study the structure of this poetry is thus to study both a sustained effort of knowledge and self-knowledge, and the identity defined and created by that effort. The poet's real identity is created by the activity of speaking forth his consciousness and its objects.

iv. *Patterns of Structure and Theme*

Two structural patterns, or kinds of movement, dominate the *Epistles to Several Persons*, the *Imitations of Horace*, and Pope's other major poems of the 1730s. On the one hand, there is the pattern of the epistles, in which schematic knowledge, usually of the distanced and satiric sort, is gradually humanized to substantial knowledge, and the poet is led from more or less severe isolation to a certain degree of involvement in a world partly redeemed. On the other hand, there is the pattern of the satires, in which substantial knowledge is gradually converted to schematic knowledge of the satiric sort, and the poet is led from a precarious but apparently substantial accord with the world to nearly total isolation. *To a Lady*, for all its tragic perception, conforms to the ultimately comic pattern of the epistles. *Satire II. i.* and the two dialogues of the *Epilogue to the Satires*, for all the exuberance of their wit, display the tragic pattern of the satires. "Comic" and "tragic," needless to say, are in no way to be equated with "cheerful" and "gloomy."

The double nature of his controlling image of man dictates the degree to which Pope's poetry participates in epistolary and satiric, and comic and tragic patterns, especially comic myths of communal identity and tragic myths of heroic solitude. Pope's task is to save that double nature by refusing to allow either impulse to subsume the other. Yet he must also avoid the indeterminacy to which merely negative resistance can lead, and which he once saw as the nature of a "true Modern Life": "One might, with much better reason, ask the same Question of a Modern Life, that Mr. Rich did of a Modern Play; *Pray do me the favor, Sir, to inform me; Is this your Tragedy or your Comedy?*"[16] The solitary vision of the tragic hero is therefore deflected toward the world, as in *An Epistle to Dr. Arbuthnot*, or when it triumphs it is first resisted, as in the *Epilogue to the Satires*. In each case, the qualification is a process, and the meaning of the poem is the meaning of its movement taken as a whole.

At times, in the epistles, schematic knowledge is qualified not by a countermovement but by sheer exaggeration: what begins as a reduction of chaos to meaningful pattern ends as a *reductio ad absurdum*, as in the discussion of "second qualities" in *To Cobham*. More often, however, there is a less direct form of the *reductio* in which a privileged moment of humanization, a kind of lyric or epistolary recognition scene, follows a moment of fantasy or schematic knowledge, a moment in which the poet or another character has attempted to subdue the particularity and chanciness of the world to the absoluteness of the mind's demands: Timon's architectural impositions (*To Burlington*); the fantasy of the Lord *in primo Georgii* (*Epistle II.ii.*); the anxious speech of Swift concerning property (*Satire II.ii.*); Pope's own fantasy of human perfection at the close of his address to Lord Bolingbroke (*Epistle I.i.*). In other poems, this point of recognition is diffused into a curve of gradual discovery.

Pope's resistance to the extremes of the comic and tragic is matched by another effort of qualification: his treatment of the heroic. In Pope's mature original poetry, the heroic image of man is most fully affirmed only in extreme situations such as that at the end of the second dialogue of the *Epilogue to the Satires*, and even there it is qualified. More often, as in the closing lines of *Epistle I.i.*, this image is affirmed, but it is also criticized for excluding so much of human nature. Elsewhere, the heroic image is pointedly introduced into homely contexts, as in the case of the Man of Ross in *To Bathurst*, or, as the portrait of the Man of Ross also illustrates, it functions as a frankly exemplary image to which conduct may aspire if not live up. The sort of heroism that Pope most fully endorses can be seen in *An Essay on Man* or, indirectly, in *The Dunciad*. The hero of these poems is man, but man only insofar as he conducts that act of self-demystification which allows his relatedness to the world to appear, only insofar as he recovers his essential humanity. This is a continual effort. Indeed, the *Essay on Man* ends with the narrator beginning again, turning from the envisaged blessedness that charity confers and toward that single friend and guide with whom, in the process of life only momentarily suspended by the poem, he must again begin to make his soul. It is the heroism of the quest for full humanity, which a heroic image may guide and to a certain degree inform, that Pope celebrates in his art.

Pope's treatment of the heroic image, therefore, depends upon his recognition that it is an image, something distinct — though perhaps fruitfully so — from the existential center of his idea of man. Pope's response to this image is thus a response to a simplification that must be recognized as such if it is to connect with a more substantial and realistic vision of human nature. In an analogous way Horace is important to Pope. In addition to providing an opportunity to consult "the Dead, and live past Ages o'er,"[17] and thus to approach a central humanity that is common to Roman and English poet alike, Horace provided a poetry in which that humanity was more accessible to the self than it is in Pope's poetry. Pope takes Horatian assumptions as an image or background against which he depicts his own struggle to achieve what Horace assumes or can achieve with greater ease: an ordered self, or the ability to endure disorder; an acceptance of the depredations of time; an understanding that the man of vision is always alienated, and therefore that vision and experience always require to be wed anew. Pope implicates elements of the apocalyptic into his Horatian originals, darkens Horace's view of politics, and stresses the burden of the poet's alienation. Pope's poetry is therefore at once more visionary and more thoroughly embedded in the particulars of its time than Horace's; the intensification at either extreme forces us to see the precariousness at its center, and to hear the poet's efforts to maintain and to speak from that center.

In Pope's way of using the heroic image and Horatian assumptions such as these we can see a pattern that is reflected in his treatment of several particularly eighteenth-century themes, a pattern in which he allows certain doctrines, formulations, maxims, and images to guide and instruct him, but never to become wholly identified with his position. This consistently skeptical or "secondary" relationship to the fixed and final is largely responsible for the impression of intellectual and moral independence projected by the speaker of his satires and epistles. The problem of the continuity of the self, for example, which had been raised in other ways by Descartes and Locke, and was soon to be exacerbated by Hume, is reflected in Pope's hypothesis of the Ruling Passion (itself a revival). The Ruling Passion assures a simple continuity of one sort, for it is an elemental force continuing from birth to death, "cast and mingl'd with our very Frame." But at the same time, Pope posits, and demonstrates, most clearly in the Horatian epistles and *An Epistle to Dr. Arbuthnot*, a complex act of self-examination, moral imagination, and sheer persistence whereby a man may achieve continuity of a higher sort by accepting and directing his Ruling Passion. This is a moral rather than a metaphysical "answer" to the problem, but it permits Pope to include in his conception of man the possibility of a resignation of the human, and to place the effort to achieve a moral identity and a stable self at the center of that conception. The simpler sort of continuity is here not unattainable, but it is only obliquely relevant to the sphere of free choice and moral identity. Like the heroic image, like the vision of the world created in Horace's epistles and satires, it must be qualified and revised before the poet can claim it as his own.

v. The Double Vision: An Essay on Man *and* The Dunciad

The epistles and satires, then, are structural opposites, one moving from schematic to substantial knowledge and the other from substantial to schematic. Each, roughly speaking, begins where the other ends, and each includes aspects of the other. The epistles and satires gesture, from their different perspectives, toward the poet's total interpretation of experience and toward his identity, and together they suggest the complexity and doubleness of that knowledge and identity. Pope strives throughout his poetry to preserve that doubleness, for only in this way can he respect the paradox at the center of his nature. This is not a matter of merely asserting that doubleness is man's appropriate mode of being, although Pope does assert this in Epistle II of *An Essay on Man* and elsewhere. It is a matter of living it, of continually recovering and preserving the double vision in the face of all the temptations posed by various forms of simplified truth. In Pope's case these are usually the temptations of schematic knowledge, of visionary satire, and of the role of One Just Man criticizing a uniformly degenerate world from a position of proud aloofness. Indeed, at times, this seems to be the only position a sane man can creditably adopt. At these times, the effort to honor the doubleness of human knowledge and identity necessarily involves the poet in acts of resistance to extremely powerful impulses, like the impulse to visionary satire that finds expression in the *Epilogue to the Satires:*

> Yet may this Verse (if such a Verse remain)
> Show there was one who held it in disdain.
> *(Epilogue to the Satires,* I. 171-72)

> Yes, I am proud; I must be proud to see
> Men not afraid of God, afraid of me.

>   Yes, the last Pen for Freedom let me draw.
>   (*Epilogue to the Satires*, II. 208-9, 248)

Such impulses must be expressed, but they must also be
resisted, for they can betray "th'unbalanc'd Mind" to one
extreme "and snatch the Man away" (*Epistle I. vi.* 24-25).[18]

   This drama of resistance and self-qualification is clearest
in those of Pope's poems where we might most expect to find
it, the introspective and conversational *Imitations of Horace*
and, to a lesser degree, the *Epistles to Several Persons*. But it is
also an important element in such apparently monumental
and un-Horatian utterances as *An Essay on Man* and *The
Dunciad* of 1743. Both poems, in very different ways,
incorporate within their affirmations a resistance to the
poet's knowledge and a validating — and in the case of *The
Dunciad*, a devastating — criticism of that knowledge. The
nature of this criticism may be suggested by the curious fact
that each poem at some point allies the writing of poetry
with the airy speculations of the alchemist. The *Essay*,
exploring the comforts peculiar to each human state, draws
the poet into a characteristically double-edged description:

>   See the blind beggar dance, the cripple sing,
>   The sot a hero, lunatic a king;
>   *The starving chemist in his golden views*
>   *Supremely blest, the poet in his muse.*
>   (II. 267-70, my emphasis)

The opening of Book Three of *The Dunciad*, perhaps more
cruelly, gathers the poet up into the fog of Bays's rapturous
vision:

>   Then raptures high the seat of sense o'erflow,
>   Which only heads, refin'd from reason, know.
>   Hence, from the straw where Bedlam's Prophet nods,
>   He hears loud Oracles, and talks with Gods:

Hence the Fool's Paradise, the Statesman's Scheme,
The air-built Castle, and the golden Dream,
The Maid's romantic wish, *the Chemist's flame,*
And Poet's vision of eternal Fame.
                                        (III. 5-12, my emphasis)

More far-reaching is the double vision whereby both
poems offer themselves as forms of epic, but epic sharply
and unmistakably qualified. The *Essay on Man,* for example,
although establishing its epic credentials through a host of
features including the breadth (and height) of its theme, the
use of epic formulas, and the pointed allusions to *Paradise
Lost,* nevertheless displays several highly untraditional
characteristics. The most obvious of these is its concerted
alliance with the "lesser genres." The poem is called *An
Essay,* an initial, tentative effort. It is composed not of books,
but of four epistles. Indeed, in a paragraph "To the Reader"
prefixed to early issues of Epistle I, Pope stressed the
connection of the poem with "the Epistolary Way of Writing"
and called attention to his deliberate choice of "this Manner,
notwithstanding his Subject was high and of dignity."[19] And
in the opening lines of the poem, Pope invokes not the
sublime agency of a celestial muse, traditional source of
inspiration to the epic poet, but the human companionship
of Lord Bolingbroke, "my St. John." This invocation has its
counterpart in Book I of *The Dunciad,* where the poet
addresses Swift by redeploying the traditional epic appeal to
that aspect, and thus name, of a god most relevant to the
situation or most acceptable to the god: "O Thou! whatever
title please thine ear,/ Dean, Drapier, Bickerstaff, or
Gulliver!" (I. 19-20). The invocation is, of course, only one
element in a dense and well-known texture of allusion that
connects *The Dunciad,* though in no simple way, with
traditional epic, particularly Vergil's *Aeneid.*[20]
   Whatever else these adaptations of epic may do, they play
a large part in a simultaneous affirmation and calling into
question of the knowledge, authority, and sublime im-

personality traditionally ascribed to the bard of epic poetry. This pattern of affirmation and questioning has its structural counterpart in a pattern shared by both the *Essay* and *The Dunciad.* Each poem, seen as a structure of knowledge, embodies a double movement: toward a form of apocalyptic vision and toward a humanizing of the poet that qualifies the authority, the absoluteness, of that vision. The *Essay* moves toward a theodicean vision of charity, a vision of the gradual widening of human love to include the whole universe:

> Wide and more wide, th'o'erflowings of the mind
> Take ev'ry creature in, of ev'ry kind;
> Earth smiles around, with boundless bounty blest,
> And Heav'n beholds its image in his breast.
> (IV. 369-72)

This moment of vision, however, is followed by a turn toward the task of living, an appeal for instruction to "my Friend, my Genius," and a shift of tone which suggests that vision is yet to be won. For this closing section is the climax not simply of the knowledge asserted by the poet in the preceding Epistles but also of the skeptical attitude toward human knowledge that has coexisted with his assertions, and of the gradual process of humanization which the thunderous and chastening bard of Epistle I has undergone. Pope speaks increasingly of "us," gradually tempers the heated reproach and ironic condescension of earlier addresses, and establishes himself by the end of the *Essay* as not simply a poet and instructor but a representative man as well.

The vision of charity, then, is not suspect or inauthentic, but it expresses only part of the poet's nature, and man does not live by vision alone. Vision must be lived as well as seen, sought in the world's time as well as wondered at in the visionary moment, and made to connect with the inglorious particulars of all that is not visionary in the poet. Between the final line of the vision and the first line of the poet's address to his friend, "Come then, my Friend, my Genius, come along," Pope recalls himself to this world, resists the absoluteness of his vision by identifying it as a provisional and guiding truth, and shows himself to be a man essaying to write about man. The epic and the visionary elements are not negated by this qualification but placed in permanent tension with it, and the resulting doubleness of the poem is the doubleness of human nature.

The Dunciad, in contrast, moves toward a satiric vision of uncreation, of the restoration of "*Night* Primaeval, and of *Chaos* old":

> Lo! thy dread Empire, CHAOS! is restor'd;
> Light dies before thy uncreating word:
> Thy hand, great Anarch! lets the curtain fall;
> And Universal Darkness buries All.
>
> (IV. 653-56)

Like *An Essay on Man*, *The Dunciad* humanizes the image of the poet in several ways, including the sudden introduction of personal address, as in the invocation to Swift, the lines to "my Paridel" (IV. 341-46), or the dramatic and personal opening of Book IV:

> Yet, yet a moment, one dim Ray of Light
> Indulge, dread Chaos, and eternal Night!
> Of darkness visible so much be lent,
> As half to shew, half veil the deep Intent.
> Ye Pow'rs! whose Mysteries restor'd I sing,
> To whom Time bears me on his rapid wing,
> Suspend a while your Force inertly strong,
> Then take at once the Poet and the Song.
>
> (IV. 1-8)

But the extremes of *The Dunciad* are more violent than those of the *Essay*. Pope envisions not the growth of the individual into charity but the eclipse of civilization; more important, he is not merely a man among men at the conclusion of the poem but perilously close to being a dunce among dunces,

"willing to approve himself a genuine Son" of Dulness, as a
note to Book IV tells us (IV. 1.n.). At the close of that book,
the poet at last acknowledges the irresistible sway of Dulness:
"In vain, in vain, — the all-composing Hour/Resistless falls:
The Muse obeys the Pow'r" (IV. 627-28).

It is possible to understand "The Muse obeys the Pow'r" in
more than one way. The phrase refers, first, to the poet's
internal state, to a felt failure of poetic force, but it refers as
well to the poem, and suggests that the succumbing of the
Muse is discoverable in lines already uttered by the poet.
This is, in fact, the case, and the relevant features of the
poem are precisely its visionary scope and the dramatic
situation which that scope implies. At the close of the poem,
as in the early lines of Book IV, Pope's poetic mode is one of
allegorical vision:

> Beneath her foot-stool, *Science* groans in Chains,
> And *Wit* dreads Exile, Penalties and Pains.
> There foam'd rebellious *Logic*, gagg'd and bound,
> There, stript, fair *Rhet'ric* languish'd on the ground;
> His blunted Arms by *Sophistry* are born,
> And shameless *Billingsgate* her Robes adorn.
>   (IV. 21-26; 27-42 continue in this mode)

> Thus at her felt approach, and secret might,
> *Art* after *Art* goes out, and all is Night.
> See skulking *Truth* to her old Cavern fled,
> Mountains of Casuistry heap'd o'er her head!
> *Philosophy*, that lean'd on Heav'n before,
> Shrinks to her second cause, and is no more.
> *Physic* of *Metaphysic* begs defence,
> And *Metaphysic* calls for aid on *Sense*!
> See *Mystery* to *Mathematics* fly!
> In vain! they gaze, turn giddy, rave, and die.
> *Religion* blushing veils her sacred fires,
> And unawares *Morality* expires.
>   (IV. 639-50)

The later passage is, first of all, an echo of the visions of
Settle in Book III, especially Settle's vision of an anti-

apocalypse, a "new world to Nature's laws unknown" (III. 235ff.). More important, Pope's vision is an instance of schematic knowledge expanded to apocalyptic scope: the world is seen as a demonic pattern, a lucid tableau of horror, uncomplicated by saving qualifications or recalcitrant details. And Pope, though he announces that "The Muse obeys the Pow'r," acts as if she did not; for he stands well above the events he describes before the final vision, and he seems to speak from this Olympian perspective during the course of the vision itself.[21] Indeed, as those visionary scenes expand to encompass the entire world of human creation, the capacities of mind and the achievements of civilization, Pope's position becomes more and more that of the satirist speaking *ab extra*, knowing and judging from a privileged position outside the world of men.

At the logical extreme of this situation, when Dulness has swallowed up all intelligence and the poet has assumed the role of One Just Man, Pope confronts a profound dilemma. On the one hand, his knowledge tells him that it is right to assume this role since all civilized intelligence but his has succumbed to Dulness. On the other hand, his posture of total alienation is nearly indistinguishable from that of the dunces who, though collectively uniform, are mad individualists when they are considered singly. There is no authority but the poet's own to distinguish his vision from paranoid fantasy nourished by pride, his heroic isolation from the alienated madness of a dunce. Lacking a world, Pope could only secure his authority by making more than human claims for it, and this he will not do. In order to respect both his Olympian vision and his limited humanity, therefore, Pope must announce that Dulness has wholly enveloped the world while he acknowledges that to say so is perhaps to make himself into the last of the dunces. He cannot avoid this dilemma and he does not. Pope is not, as some readers have urged, secretly in sympathy with the repose offered by Dulness.[22] He is, however, inevitably allied with her company of followers by the very gap that separates him from the world of men, by the very absoluteness of his vision of a world in ruins.

The cost of this vision is apparent. At the close of *The Dunciad*, when Pope acknowledges that "The Muse obeys the Pow'r," he also acknowledges that his vision has cost him the world it has seen through. He is left alone to address Dulness, who is the audience of the closing lines. Yet Pope is not simply a tragic hero who, having gradually isolated himself, at last accepts his isolation and confirms it as his choice. This view is only half the truth. The other half of Pope's strategy is precisely to resist these heroics, to intimate that his "inhuman" isolation is related to duncelike eccentricity and that the absolute vision which perfectly isolates him from the "vast involuntary throng" also, at last, unites him to it. It is not possible to simplify this doubleness, to decide that Pope is "at last" a tragic hero or "at last" a comic victim; he is both. And in his insistence on being both, Pope raises to its highest pitch his lifelong belief that man is, at his most essential and genuine, "a being darkly wise," "created half to rise and half to fall;/ Great lord of all things, yet a prey to all."[23] In his effort to preserve this double condition, Pope as strenuously resists the singleness of proud and isolated knowledge as the singleness of mere unthinking complicity in the way of the world.

vi. *The Quest for Substantial Knowledge, 1728-1743*

In his Preface of 1717 Pope had written: "I declare I shall think the world in the right, and quietly submit to every truth which time shall discover to the prejudice of these writings; *not so much as wishing so irrational a thing, as that every body should be deceiv'd, meerly for my credit*" (my emphasis). At the close of Book IV of *The Dunciad*, when Pope submits to the world he has satirically mastered, he fulfills this promise. He performs his final act of resistance by refusing to separate the truth of the visionary from that of the man, or the truth of the self from that of the world in which it must, inevitably, live.

If we can see *An Essay on Man* and *The Dunciad* as poems that incorporate an act of resistance to the poetic knowledge they also assert in order to lend that knowledge substantiality, then we may be able to see the *Epistles to Several Persons* and *Imitations of Horace* as more overt explorations of knowledge and strategies of resistance. In the *Epistles to Several Persons*, beginning with *To Burlington* in 1731, Pope first explores at length the problems of knowledge that shape the poems of the 1730s. In the Horatian epistles, which focus on the poet himself, problems of knowledge are largely problems of self-knowledge, and the poet strives to move beyond schematic images to a substantial apprehension of his own nature. In the satires, Pope turns outward to confront the world. Schematic and substantial knowledge, in this expanded context, widen to become apocalyptic vision and historical understanding. It is possible, finally, to see Pope's major poetry of the 1730s as an extended act of resistance to the apocalyptic knowledge that first thrusts itself upon him in *The Dunciad* of 1728 but which is fully expressed, and fully resisted, only in the four-book *Dunciad* of 1743. In the poems of this period, Pope assumes the role of representative man, striving to come to terms with — to reconcile, but also to value and sustain — those fertile human contradictions which the situation of the poet exacerbates and clarifies, and at the center of which lies his complex and paradoxical identity.

Pope's later poetry, and his greatest, is concerned with problems of knowledge and vision. The poet attempts to do justice to powers of vision that threaten to deprive both world and self of their substantiality, and to other forces within the self that resist this vision, that offer to know the world in such a way that it might be inhabited as well as comprehended. Yet since every new formulation threatens to harden into rigidity and to falsify the precarious doubleness of the self, Pope's dilemma must be repeatedly met with imaginative strategies of only provisional potency. Freedom must be found within necessity; a possible world within an impossible kingdom of corruption and dullness; substance within mere scheme; and vital time within lifeless cycle, or within a demonic time that is merely the medium in which repugnant patterns work themselves out. The poems must therefore be read with attention to their temporal structure, for they are not statements but dramatizations, efforts of recovery and resistance. The answers they offer to the dilemmas that Pope faces do not reside in isolable formulations, but in the exemplary dramas of moral and imaginative discovery that lend the poems their structure and meaning and shape the identity of the poet.

2 Human Knowledge and Poetic Structure

i. *Introduction:* Epistles to Several Persons

AN Essay on Man and *The Dunciad* significantly resist their visions even as they express them, but the main thrust of each poem is nevertheless toward one of two extremes, two kinds of total vision or cosmic myth: theodicean in *An Essay on Man*, satiric in *The Dunciad.* The *Epistles to Several Persons* stand between these extremes. They are, to be sure, concerned with instances of charity and dullness, but they do not offer comprehensive visions, either theodicean or satiric. The focus of the *Epistles to Several Persons* is on the intricacies of the poet's relations with other individuals and on his scrutiny of scenes less extensive than the world. Instead of presenting cosmic myths, they entertain possible stances, possible ways of knowing those individuals and those scenes. Indeed, although the acts of knowledge they embody are less dramatic and visionary than those of *An Essay on Man* or *The Dunciad,* the *Epistles to Several Persons* nevertheless participate as insistently as either of those poems in the quest for a substantial interpretation of the world.

To claim that the *Epistles to Several Persons* are primarily about knowledge may seem to claim too much. They are, of course, about true and false taste, the use of riches, the characters of men and women. Yet having said this, we must also say that the subjects of these poems are no more important than their structures, and that these structures are, in the case of all four epistles, chiefly significant as acts

37

of knowledge. *To a Lady,* for example, is about the characters of women; but the real significance of the poem is the way in which it dramatizes the poet's growth from mere schematic knowledge into a substantial understanding of female and human character. This poem is as profoundly "about" the problem of knowing the characters of women as it is about the characters of women in themselves. Similarly, *To Bathurst* is about the use of riches, but its chief significance is that it strives to win Bathurst to a different way of knowing the world, a way that will permit him to discover possibility and significance in it and thus to "teach us" by means of his good works. Bathurst must come to know the world so as to grant it substantiality and humanity without minimizing its massive corruption and horror. This is a difficult task, but his human survival depends on it. These problems of knowledge center on correctly knowing and valuing the world; they are problems in the interpretation of experience.

The initial emphasis of the *Epistles to Several Persons* is satiric. Each epistle opens with a satiric rejection of some kind (only in one case by the poet) and with a reductive account of what is being rejected: the trifling virtuosos of the world of taste in *To Burlington*; the world of men itself in *To Bathurst,* populated as it is — for Lord Bathurst — by "the standing jest of Heav'n" (4); two kinds of man and two kinds of knowledge in *To Cobham*; and the characters of women in *To a Lady*: " 'Most Women have no Characters at all' " (2). Since Pope's deepest commitment in these poems, however, is to substantiality and doubleness, to the mixed condition of real life, the dramas that develop from those openings are frequently shaped by the discovery of counterinstances and recalcitrant examples that qualify and deepen the satiric schemes by which the world is initially known. If these instances and examples do not themselves constitute a theodicean scheme or reconciling myth, it is because the very process of qualification in which they participate implies a resistance to the sweep and simplification of schemes and myths, satiric or nonsatiric. Theodicy in the full sense makes only a fleeting appearance in Pope's epistles, but insofar as showing one's world to be livable is the secondary goal of theodicy, these poems are secondary theodicies.[1]

These counterexamples do at times cohere into a recognizable myth. In some cases, it is genuinely theodicean, as in *An Essay on Man*; in others, it is heroic and national, as in *Windsor Forest* or (more skeptically) in *To Burlington* and the late fragment, *Brutus*; in still others, the myth is rural and Horatian, as in the early "Ode on Solitude" and the later *Imitations of Horace*.[2] Usually, however, these myths prove inadequate. The 1728 *Dunciad* suggests how tenable the national aspirations of *Windsor Forest* proved to be. The retirement myth is more durable and its fate more complex, but it becomes increasingly problematic. Retirement first presents itself to Pope as an intermediate state between full participation in the world and total withdrawal from it. But participation and withdrawal come to be seen not as extremes of a spectrum but as mutually exclusive and equally unacceptable alternatives. The situation thus created is, to simplify, a dilemma of an excluded middle. Retirement also, at last, proves untenable. Moreover, such myths — indeed, all myths — contain the seeds of their own inadequacy within their very ability to account for the phenomena of experience. As they acquire coherence and stability, they may become increasingly dangerous, for they may begin to mimic the lifeless coherence of those myths of different import which they were created to resist.

Thus, although the *Epistles to Several Persons* strive to resist the satiric schemes with which they open, they also reveal an increasing skepticism toward the possibility — indeed, the desirability — of fashioning a reconciling countermyth. Taken in their order of composition, they turn from the broad possibility of a heroic national myth to the more limited actuality of individual characters whose richness and coherence of spirit show them to be supreme instances of humanity. Real figures, in the world of the poem, they also acquire a symbolic significance. Pope turns the quest for a reconciling myth into a continually renewed search for central principles of human nature, and these principles are to be found embodied not in nation or world but in individuals. There is an undeniable loss of scope in this: *To Burlington* closes with a vision, however qualified, of "Imperial Works"; *To a Lady,* with a vision of the poet's friend. At the same time, there is an undeniable gain in reality, for the friend indeed exists, while the "Imperial works" are only envisioned.

Moreover, both the project that Pope outlines at the close of *To Burlington* and the character of the friend to whom he pays tribute in *To a Lady* participate, in their different ways, in what might be called a deromanticized conception of humanity, of human service and human worth. Figures such as Lord Burlington and the Lady display a particularly homely and unextravagant kind of heroism. They illustrate the ways in which the pressure of the grand or heroic may be brought to bear on the forms of common life, and in doing so they sharpen our sensitivity to the unexpected dignity of the quotidian. Characters like these are part of Pope's effort to replace the unifying power of a heroic image of man or nation with the discovery of authentic humanity in the life about him, and thus to recall us to the dignity and seriousness of the business of living. "He passed through common life," Johnson says, "sometimes vexed and sometimes pleased, with the natural emotions of common men."[3]

Several features of this effort specifically concern poetry. First, Pope indirectly affirms that the common life of men and women is a suitable poetic subject. In thus deromanticizing the heroism of poetic characters, he deromanticizes the figure of the poet as well. Pope is not a heroic bard hymning imperial conquests and superhuman characters (whether warriors or statesmen), but chiefly a discoverer, brooding on scenes of common life in search of those points at which the genuinely human may be significantly apprehended. Throughout the 1730s, Pope's poetry suggests that the poet is an exemplary man who is defined by his effort to perform this task of discovery. In the *Imitations of Horace*, Pope goes further to become not only a discoverer but also the character, however unlikely, in whom that genuine humanity may be discovered.

To connect the high calling of poetry in this way with the material of common life is not simply to exalt that material but to ground and substantialize poetry as well, to affirm its importance in human life. At times, Pope himself seems to question this importance. "If I was to begin the world again," he tells Spence in 1730, "and knew just what I do now, I would never write a verse."[4] We may share Johnson's skepticism toward such remarks: "He considered poetry as the business of his life, and, however he might seem to lament his occupation, he followed it with constancy: to make verses was his first labour, and to mend them was his last."[5] But we may also believe that Pope's remarks express a temperament concerned not only to write poetry but also to justify it by disclosing its connections with common life. Pope's resistance to the decorum separating the poet from the subjects of common life (except insofar as they were considered satirically) was the special literary form of his resistance to the schematic knowledge separating him from the world, a resistance dramatized throughout the poetry of the 1730s.

From a historical standpoint, this was more than a personal problem; the need for a justification of poetry was hardly Pope's alone. His assertion in *An Epistle to Dr. Arbuthnot* — "I left no Calling for this idle trade,/ No Duty broke, no Father dis-obey'd" (129-30) — was indeed addressed to Arbuthnot, and to himself, but it was addressed also to the current of skepticism that had led Locke's *Some Thoughts Concerning Education* through nine editions by 1732. "If he have a Poetick Vein," Locke writes of the budding infant, " 'tis to me the strangest thing in the World that the Father should desire or suffer it to be cherished or improved. . . . I know not what Reason a Father can have to wish his Son a Poet, who does not desire to have him bid Defiance to all other Callings and Business." The strongest "reason" had been given earlier by Locke himself: "Every one's natural Genius should be carry'd as far as it could."[6]

Locke does not seem troubled by the contradiction, but it is an important one to Pope. For the poet's special apartness, the distance from the world that his vision enforces and against which he must continually struggle without wholly collapsing it, is in Pope a metaphor for the alienation of the individual from substantial knowledge and substantial experience.[7] This alienation could be conceived as tragic. Locke's remarks, although he does not mean to convey this, might even be read as a statement of the cost of such individuality as the poet enjoys. Pope, however, was determined not to suffer this cost, for he believed that it rested on a false separation of genius and humanity, poet and man, books and business. He strove throughout his later career to unite these opposed terms. When he could not do so, he attempted to respect them equally, to insist on the difficult doubleness of the poetic identity they helped to constitute and, therefore, of the poet's relationship to the world.

Pope's effort to discover connections — or to discover a mode of knowledge hospitable to the discovery of connections — between the poet of individual genius and the recalcitrant world he must inhabit takes the form of specific literary techniques. First, he makes knowledge itself an important theme. The knowledge upon which judgments of the world are based is not simply presupposed but is treated explicitly as a problem. Immediate judgments of "knave" or "fool" are qualified; others' motives are analyzed and compared with the poet's own; and the depths of character beneath behavior are closely examined. The aberrant, as a result, is to a certain degree humanized, while the aberrant or idiosyncratic tendencies of the normal are more fully acknowledged. Pope's techniques of portraiture also become more complex. The structure of the portrait of Timon in *To Burlington*, for example, is, roughly speaking, deductive: it develops a character from a few initial principles. This is not the case with the more significant portraits in *To a Lady*, in which the initial "principles of explanation" are qualified as the portrait proceeds, and the initial aloofness of the poet toward the women modulates to more sympathetic under-standing. Detached portrayal moves, in effect, closer to complex encounter. The potential rigidity of the satiric role, its necessary yet perilous sundering of self from world, its tendency toward proud aloofness — these are countered with a more generous awareness, a humane self-consciousness which the rigors of a critical role seem to call up as their necessary qualification. This humane self-consciousness confirms the poet's membership in the world of men and women that his genius leads him to scan and measure.

The *Epistles to Several Persons* were first published separately in the order of their composition — *To Burlington, To Bathurst, To Cobham, To a Lady* (IV, III, I, II) — and were collected for the 1735 Works, Volume II, in what has come to be their present order: *To Cobham, To a Lady, To Bathurst, To Burlington* (I, II, III, IV). F. W. Bateson remarks with some truth that "the order in which these poems are printed — that in which most of us tend, perhaps wrongly, to read them — was entirely determined by the requirements of the almost non-existent '*Opus Magnum.*' "[8] But Bateson's "entirely" is too emphatic. The Works order (I, II, III, IV) may have been determined in part, even in large part, by the requirements of the *Opus Magnum* but it is difficult to believe that Pope would not also have demanded that this order make good artistic sense, in or out of the *Opus Magnum*. Just a month after *To Bathurst* appeared, Pope touched on this question in a letter to Swift: "I have declined opening to you by letters the whole scheme of my present Work, expecting still to do it in a better manner in person: but you will see pretty soon, that the letter to Lord Bathurst is a part of it, and you will find a plain connexion between them, if you read them in the order just contrary to that they were published in."[9] The "present Work," no doubt, is the projected *Opus Magnum,* but the "them" between which there is "a plain connexion" seems clearly to refer to the two already published *Epistles to Several Persons*. Pope, therefore, is urging Swift to read them in the order in which they appeared in the 1735 Works: *To Bathurst, To Burlington.*

There is, in fact, sound thematic logic in the Works order. Beginning with *To Cobham* and concluding with *To Burlington,* the four epistles move from an intensely individual focus — indeed, from the suggestion that each of us may be locked into something like a solipsistic prison — to a vision of national possibility intimating that a heroic image of king and nation might yet be recaptured. Coexisting with this expanding focus, moreover, is another pattern, which governs the two pairs of poems into which the *Epistles to Several Persons* readily fall: *To Cobham* and *To a Lady, To Bathurst* and *To Burlington.* The first poem in each pair raises problems that achieve more concrete and adequate resolution in the second poem. The portrait of the friend in *To a Lady,* for example, concludes not only that poem but the entire discussion of the knowledge of character initiated by *To Cobham.* This portrait dissolves the various strategies for knowing the character of another — observation, historical reconstruction, application of the hypothesis of the Ruling Passion — into a substantial apprehension of the Friend's rich nature. Similarly, the question of the proper use of wealth, which is also a question of how one may participate virtuously in the life of nation and world, is raised and worried in *To Bathurst* but achieves a relatively satisfying answer only in the last portion of *To Burlington*. Highly imperfect solutions and a high proportion of abstract theorizing give way to greater certainty and greater concreteness.

These pairings, however, exist in both orderings of the *Epistles to Several Persons*, although *To Bathurst* and *To Burlington* are reversed, as are the pairs themselves. In the compositional order (IV, III, I, II), a further pattern is introduced, that of "constructive renunciation," which Maynard Mack has shown to govern the unfolding of *An Essay on Man*.[10] *To Burlington* and *To Bathurst* record the breakdown of the idea of national greatness and "Imperial Works," and the growth of a profoundly skeptical and satiric attitude toward the world. At the same time, they dramatize the dangers of such an attitude, its capacity to dull human responses and undermine character. *To Cobham* attempts, by means of the Ruling Passion, to construct another way of knowing that world, but it also points up the inadequacy of this effort. *To a Lady* takes *To Cobham* further, revising its categories and dramatizing the progression from schematic to substantial knowledge. In doing so, it both reenacts and brings to completion the movement of the poet's consciousness through the four epistles. The chief significance of the poem thus lies in the exemplary educative process undergone by the poet himself. In *To a Lady* as in the *Epistles to Several Persons* taken as a whole, the skeptical imagination, brooding on trivial surfaces, is gradually led onward to a fuller humanity and a more fully humanized art.

Traditional literary history, whatever its scope, is the invention of fictions of continuity, causal connections between discrete points (works, authors, periods). Our preference for one fiction over another is, or ought to be, guided by the completeness and elegance of its formulation, by the kind of sense it makes. It is evident from Pope's career that the

vision of national possibility articulated in *Windsor Forest*
came increasingly to be replaced with a vision closer to that
of *The Dunciad*. Pope continually resisted this satiric
absoluteness, but his effort of resistance only complicated
the pattern of skepticism; it did not eliminate it. To read the
Epistles to Several Persons in the order in which they appeared
in the 1735 Works is thus to see them as the single exception
to the overall pattern of Pope's career from (at least) 1713 to
1743. To read these poems in their order of composition is to
see them as fitting into that pattern and helping to articulate
it. This is not to say that the very presence of two orders is
not a significant fact, nor is it to deny that the rearrangement
of the four epistles into the Works order may itself have been
a form of resistance, however oblique. It is simply to choose
as an object of criticism the structure that makes the best
sense.

ii. *"Something like Prophetic strain"*: To Burlington

The epistle *To Burlington* (1731) is the first poem Pope
published after *The Dunciad Variorum* (1729). In the later
poem, Pope moves away from the visionary satire of *The
Dunciad* and strives to recover as much of his earlier vision of
georgic possibility, seen most clearly in *Windsor Forest,* as
later experience will permit. An important feature of the
georgic poem is its creation of a vital civic present. It
conceives of the present as a center of energy capable of
holding together past and future, origin and destiny, just as
it conceives of a social order capable of holding together
rural pursuits and imperial aspirations. The literary form of
the tensions that georgic sustains may be seen in its
combination of historical myth and prophecy. In *Windsor
Forest,* for example, the myth of Lodona and the prophecy of
Father Thames infuse the present British countryside with a
sense of origin and destiny, the gentle Loddon adding its

modest energies to the envisaged sweep of "unbounded Thames."

These myths and prophecies are made continuous with a realistic present. When Father Thames predicts that "Thy Trees, fair *Windsor*! now shall leave their Woods,/ And half thy Forests rush into my Floods" (385-86), he echoes the poet, who had said, in a lower key, much the same thing earlier in the poem:

> Thou too, great Father of the *British* Floods!
> With joyful Pride survey'st our lofty Woods,
> Where tow'ring Oaks their growing Honours rear,
> And future Navies on thy Shores appear.
>
> (219-22)

The visionary prophecy has been rooted in the actual landscape; it articulates the possibility inherent in concrete fact. Father Thames' very appearance is similarly connected to historical reality, for it is Queen Anne's *fiat pax* that liberates the British Genius:

> At length great *Anna* said — let Discord cease!
> She said, the World obey'd, and all was *Peace*!
> In that blest Moment, from his Oozy Bed
> Old Father *Thames* advanc'd his rev'rend Head.
>
> (327-30)

As G. Wilson Knight has written: "Deep submission to nature is felt expanding into communal and national prophecy. . . . Oaks are 'future navies' (222), with no straining of association. . . . The generalizing tendency never loses contact with perceptual impressions."[11] Each reader must decide whether there is a "straining of association," but there is much thematic and structural evidence that Pope grounded his mythology firmly in the earth.[12]

In *Windsor Forest*, then, the social order asserts present achievement as the earnest of future greatness. It stands between the individual and the imperium, the past and the future; and assures a happy translation of energies. In the epistle *To Burlington*, this is no longer the case. Apart from the closing section, there is no suggestion of an order able to accept individual energies and lend them larger significance. The present is a tableau of satiric examples. Burlington's "noble rules" will "Fill half the land with Imitating Fools" (25-26). The Aristotelian notion of "Magnificence" requires a context larger than the personal, but the view from the present in the moral world of the poem is much like the view from Timon's garden: "On ev'ry side you look, behold the Wall!" (114). It is possible to take a larger view of the present, noting that Timon's pride inadvertently assists the poor (169-72); but this view supplies only social consolation, not a social role, and the central questions raised by *To Burlington* are: Where can the virtuous individual (here, the artist) find the private in the public good? How can he interpret his own time so as to participate substantially in it? It seems, for much of the poem, that the artist cannot, that he is condemned to an adversary posture. The world of *To Burlington* lacks the vital civic present that held together the various orders, both temporal and hierarchical, in *Windsor Forest* by mediating individual labors in the direction of the imperial dream.

The need for the critical stance of the adversary is not so much discussed as assumed and demonstrated in the first four fifths of the poem, and two features of the present in Pope's satiric account are particularly striking: it is transparent, and it is static. Both of these features contribute to the alienated coolness of the speaker's tone. "'Tis strange," the poem begins, but nothing is really strange. Like a prophet revealing the workings of that satricially inclined god who rules the sphere of Taste, Pope cuts through surfaces to reveal pattern:

> For what has Virro painted, built, and planted?
> Only to show, how many Tastes he wanted.

What brought Sir Visto's ill got wealth to waste?
Some Daemon whisper'd, "Visto! have a Taste."
Heav'n visits with a Taste the wealthy fool,
And needs no Rod but Ripley with a Rule.
See! sportive fate, to punish aukward pride,
Bids Bubo build, and sends him such a Guide:
A standing sermon, at each year's expense,
That never Coxcomb reach'd Magnificence!

(13-22)

The world is a book of truths all too easily read: "See!" "Behold!" And each truth reveals that the wise man who can read it has no place there.

In such a world, time is without purpose; it is merely the medium in which a pattern of folly or failure works itself out. "Villario's ten-years toil," the generations of Sabinus, the "desertion" of Nero's terraces, the inevitable trivialization of Burlington's designs — these are not true histories but exempla. Genuine time, a medium of growth rather than repetition, development rather than static pattern, appears nowhere in Pope's survey of the world of Taste except in his dramatized "advice," where the forward thrust of the verse catches the creative time it describes (57-70):

Still follow Sense, of ev'ry Art the Soul,
Parts answ'ring parts shall slide into a whole,
Spontaneous beauties all around advance,
Start ev'n from Difficulty, strike from Chance;
Nature shall join you, Time shall make it grow
A Work to wonder at — perhaps a Stow.

(65-70)

The supreme example of the transparent and static is Timon's villa. Grounds, building, library, chapel, and dinner each reveal the same thing: Timon's pride, his creation of "a new world to Nature's laws unknown."[13] "No pleasing Intricacies intervene,/ No artful wildness to perplex the scene" (115-16). Time, as a result, is fully dehumanized: "And now the Chapel's silver bell you hear" (141); "But hark! the chiming Clocks to dinner call" (151); "You drink by measure, and to minutes eat" (158). Time is merely additive, the medium of that acquisitive pride that has created a villa in its own image. Timon and his world grotesquely invert Hopkins' lines:

> Each mortal thing does one thing and the same . . .
> Selves — goes itself; *myself* it speaks and spells,
> Crying *What I do is me: for that I came*.[14]

The movement of Pope's dramatized visit is telling. It begins in the mode of voluntary and mocking survey that Pope had used in the other satiric portraits: "At Timon's Villa let us pass a day" (99). Pope ridicules the ludicrous scale of Timon's "Quarry," its inconvenience to him, and its sterility and symmetry from a perspective that recalls the Olympian stance of earlier passages (e.g., 13-22). But as the "day" progresses, Timon's villa becomes more and more, in W. H. Auden's phrase, a "coercive castle."[15] The villa begins to absorb the visitor's agency, to control him. Gardens "call" your admiration; Timon "turns you round" to the dated backs of his books; the bell "summons" you; chiming clocks "call." "Who but must laugh," Pope had remarked earlier (107), but laughter is increasingly difficult. The mocking eye is now "the suff'ring eye"; you must "sweat" through the length of the terrace, and drag your thighs "up ten steep slopes"; when you arrive, "gaping Tritons spew to wash your face." And when Pope sums up the visit, he shifts from "you" to "I," from the distance of the satiric observer, articulating a more than personal perspective, to the violence of the outraged victim, thrust back into himself by the sheer oppressiveness of what he had earlier contemned:

> In plenty starving, tantaliz'd in state,
> And complaisantly help'd to all I hate,
> Treated, caress'd, and tir'd, I take my leave,

> Sick of his civil Pride from Morn to Eve:
> I curse such lavish cost, and little skill,
> And swear no day was ever past so ill.
>
> (163-68)[16]

At this point, as his footnote tells us, Pope shifts to "the *Moral* of the whole":

> Yet hence the Poor are cloath'd, the Hungry fed;
> Health to himself, and to his Infants bread
> The Lab'rer bears: What his hard Heart denies,
> His charitable Vanity supplies.
>
> (169-72)

What is most striking about the passage is its curious roughness. The rhyme words in the first couplet, as is typical with Pope, are different parts of speech; but the lines are not grammatically parallel and the enjambment is otiose yet obtrusive. The effect is uncharacteristically awkward. (cf. 163-64, 167-68). Moreover, though parallelism is restored in the second couplet, further confusion is introduced by "his," which seems initially to refer to the laborer. And, finally, "bears" is oddly used. It is far more appropriate to "bread" than to "health," and makes for a particularly flat — a particularly "pointless" — instance of Pope's usually pointed zeugma: for example, "To rest, the Cushion and soft Dean invite" (149).

There is meaning in this difficulty. These verses constitute a theodicean bridge between satiric reductiveness and complex apprehension, between an intensely personal and a more generously universal perspective. Their awkwardness makes us feel the strain of the shift. Pope seems to emerge from Timon's as from an underworld descent, still blinking, into the light of a more inclusive vision, and at this point the poem moves into an entirely new mode. The static and satiric perspective is abandoned for a substantial vision that perceives genuine time in the world, an unfolding drama rather than a cautionary pageant:

> Another age shall see the golden Ear
> Imbrown the Slope, and nod on the Parterre,
> Deep Harvests bury all his pride has plann'd,
> And laughing Ceres re-assume the land.
>
> (173-76)

Pope's vision now includes the georgic man who enjoys "His Father's Acres" and purposefully intends them for "future Buildings, future Navies" (188), for a time when the soil will be graced or improved by the man "Who plants like Bathurst, or who builds like Boyle" (177-78). This shift in vision is matched by a heightening of style from satiric desciption and satiric "curse" (167) to hopeful vision, blessing, exhortation, and prophecy. The poem has, in effect, begun again.

The full significance of this new beginning appears only in the closing vision:

> You too proceed! make falling Arts your care,
> Erect new wonders, and the old repair,
> Jones and Palladio to themselves restore,
> And be whate'er Vitruvius was before:
> Till Kings call forth th'Idea's of your mind,
> Proud to accomplish what such hands design'd,
> Bid Harbors open, public Ways extend,
> Bid Temples, worthier of the God, ascend;
> Bid the broad Arch the dang'rous Flood contain,
> The Mole projected break the roaring Main;
> Back to his bounds their subject Sea command,
> And roll obedient Rivers through the Land;
> These Honours, Peace to happy Britain brings,
> These are Imperial Works, and worthy Kings.
>
> (191-204)

The passage is first of all a tribute to Burlington, and an exhortation to persistence in his works. It is also an attempt to reunite those terms held together by a civic order in *Windsor Forest.* These terms are held together here by nothing more than prophetic vision founded on hope, on "a courageous refusal," as T. R. Edwards says, "to forsake an ideal simply because fact seemed hostile to its fulfillment."[17] Pope's refusal is indeed courageous, but it is also the triumph of hope over experience. The momentum of the passage, its increasing tendency to sever its grammatical dependence on the provisional "Till," and the heightening of diction force one to ask whether the georgic figure and the rare instances of genuine art in the poem (The works of Bathurst, Boyle, Cobham) can support this vision; whether Pope's prophecy is grounded in the actual landscape, as it was in *Windsor Forest*, or is mere hopeful fantasy; whether, in short, the "prophetic" in these lines can survive the "strain."

These questions find one sort of answer in the nature of Pope's "Imperial Works." It has often been noted that the closing lines of the poem echo the prophecy of Anchises in Dryden's version of the sixth book of the *Aeneid*; they do not, however, echo it very faithfully. Anchises rejects one sort of achievement for another, which it will be Rome's particular destiny to accomplish:

> "Let others better mold the running mass
> Of metals, and inform the breathing brass,
> And soften into flesh a marble face;
> Plead better at the bar; describe the skies,
> And when the stars descend, and when they rise.
> But, Rome! 'tis thine alone, with awful sway,
> To rule mankind, and make the world obey:
> Disposing peace and war thy own majestic way.
> To tame the proud, the fettered slave to free,
> These are imperial arts, and worthy thee."
>
> (1168-77)

Dryden's Anchises is clearly not the Pope of *To Burlington*, but is much closer to the Father Thames of *Windsor Forest*:

> I see, I see where two fair Cities bend
> Their ample bow, a new *White-Hall* ascend!
> There mighty Nations shall inquire their Doom,

> The World's great Oracle in Times to come;
> There Kings shall sue, and suppliant States be seen
> Once more to bend before a *British* Queen.
>   Thy Trees, fair *Windsor*! now shall leave their Woods,
> And half thy Forests rush into my Floods,
> Bear *Britain*'s Thunder, and her Cross display,
> To the bright Regions of the rising Day.
>
> (379-88)

Anchises and Father Thames share a certain imperial gusto that is absent from Pope's prophecy in *To Burlington*, which is concerned with taming wild nature rather than "the proud," and which subjects the imperial myth to the sober eye of Use.

Pope thus both alludes to Dryden's Vergil and revises it. His speech fuses Anchises' two-part address ("Let others... 'tis thine") into a double perspective that rejects imperial arts for public works while nevertheless investing those works with the full dignity that Anchises accords to "awful sway." As the lines from Father Thames's speech suggest, Pope's exhortation is in one sense also a "revision" of *Windsor Forest*, a shearing away of the earlier imperial myth in favor of a more homely and durable — a less romantic — conception of national dignity and national achievement. It is also, quite literally, a revision of *To Burlington*. The version of Pope's final speech in the earlier Devonshire MS is quite close to the text we are studying, but its penultimate couplet (which appears in no other version of the poem) is highly revealing:

> Till Tyber stoop to Thames and his White hall
> Rise with the fortune of Romes Capitol.[18]

The final couplet, in the published version, remains the same — "These Honours, Peace to happy Britain brings,/ These are Imperial Works, and worthy Kings" — but it no longer carries the note of "imperial sway." The revision is complete.

Finally, and most important, revision operates in a third context, distinct from literary history and from Pope's own literary history: the context of the poem itself. One difference between the poem's closing vision and what has preceded it is suggested by the picture of nature it paints:

> Bid the broad Arch the *dang'rous Flood* contain,
> The Mole projected break the *roaring Main*;
> *Back to its bounds* their subject Sea command,
> And roll obedient Rivers thro' the Land.
>
> (199-202; my emphasis)

This is a more fierce and unruly nature than we have thus far seen, a nature whose power, like that of "laughing Ceres," is refreshing after the sterility of Timon's gardens, but also threatening in a way that Ceres is not. It is a nature that must be struggled with as well as coaxed, that challenges as much as it invigorates. In thus frankly invoking this vision of nature, Pope submits the values that inform his poetic knowledge, his vision of civilization and art — indeed, his poem — to the qualification of that larger order that will genially "bury" all that Timon's pride has planned. For this is a natural order, and to prescribe limits to it is an act of pride and folly. Pope brings to bear on the constructive power of the mind itself, on its ability to create an order that it can inhabit, a criticism which authenticates that power by imagining its limits and recognizing an order beyond them.

The body of the poem supports this interpretation, for it is concerned with disorders of the imagination, particularly with the tendency of the imagination to create self-enclosed worlds and destroy awareness. At the most innocent level, there is Sabinus:

> Thro' his young Woods how pleas'd Sabinus stray'd,
> Or sat delighted in the thick'ning shade,
> With annual joy the red'ning shoots to greet,
> Or see the stretching branches long to meet!
>
> (89-92)

It is a humorous portrait, but the line separating Sabinus from his woods has nevertheless an Ovidian shiftiness. "Annual joy," for example, or "greet," seem to arborize Sabinus as much as "Or see the stretching branches long to meet" humanizes the trees. Sabinus is not Spenser's Fradubio, transformed into a tree by Duessa's magic, yet one feels that for his metamorphosis a weaker spell might have sufficed.[19] At a less innocent level there is Timon, whose villa — though far grander than Sabinus's groves — is no less self-contained. It is a world not merely "to Nature's laws unknown" but, like Milton's Pandaemonium, an inversion of that Nature, "with a heav'n its own" (*The Dunciad*, III.242):

> On painted Cielings you devoutly stare,
> Where sprawl the Saints of Verrio or Laguerre,
> On gilded clouds in fair expansion lie,
> And bring all Paradise before your eye.
>
> (145-48)

And it is governed by thoroughly Miltonic laws of scale:

> Behold a wonder! they but now who seem'd
> In bigness to surpass Earth's Giant Sons
> Now less than smallest Dwarfs.
>
> (*P.L.* I.777-79)

> To compass this, his building is a Town,
> His pond an Ocean, his parterre a Down:
> Who but must laugh, the Master when he sees,
> A puny insect, shiv'ring at a Breeze!
>
> (105-8)

These inhabitants of private worlds, like others in the poem, seem at first to have little connection with the poet. Yet it is difficult to ignore the shift in mode after the visit to Timon, and the striking picture of nature in the closing vision. And it is more difficult to ignore the resulting qualification of Pope's earlier perspective, the difference in scope, in openness and flexibility, between:

> For what has Virro painted, built, and planted?
> Only to show, how many Tastes he wanted.
> What brought Sir Visto's ill got wealth to waste?
> Some Daemon whisper'd, "Visto! have a Taste."
> Heav'n visits with a Taste the wealthy fool,
> And needs no Rod but Ripley with a Rule.
> See! sportive fate, to punish aukward pride,
> Bids Bubo build, and sends him such a Guide:
> A standing sermon, at each year's expense,
> That never Coxcomb reach'd Magnificence!
>
> (13-22)

And:

> His Father's Acres who enjoys in peace,
> Or makes his Neighbours glad, if he encrease;
> Whose chearful Tenants bless their yearly toil,
> Yet to their Lord owe more than to the soil....
>
> (181-84)

In the earlier passage, as in the first four fifths of the poem, there is a strict discontinuity between "us" (Pope, Burlington, the judicious reader) and "them" (the citizens of that lucid satiric tableau from which the poet draws his examples). In the last section of the poem, Pope enters a larger world. Moreover, he grants that world a measure of indeterminacy, of inscrutability, of density and chanciness, that points up the simplistic neatness of his earlier formulations. In revising (though not annihilating) that earlier stance, in turning from private works to public, from a static to a temporal vision, from inflexible satire to hopeful if uncertain prophecy, and from schematic to substantial knowledge, Pope achieves a self-transcendence that is also an acknowledgment of fallibility.

For the world is a lucid book of satiric exempla only to the man who does not genuinely inhabit it. When Pope moves from his Olympian observation post into that world (Timon's), he finds it both worse and not so bad as he had imagined. It is more intensely discomforting than it had seemed, but it is

not so uniformly bad. Despite the tone of universal disgust
early in the poem, the sense that no matter where one looked
things were the same, the experience of Timon's villa shows
that they are not. Real differences still exist in the world,
both within the present ("Yet hence the Poor are cloath'd . . . .")
and between present and future ("Another age shall see . . . .").
It is the restoration of this sense of difference — a restoration
of substantiality to a world that had seemed mere pattern —
that marks Pope's growth of vision, and that distinguishes
him from those characters whose worlds consist, unqualifiedly,
of reflected ego. The naive pastoral harmony of self and
world in the case of Sabinus or the ruthless imposition of
such a harmony by sheer will in the case of Timon
characterize minds that are at once too close to, and too far
from, experience. Sabinus and Timon are perfectly at home
in their worlds, but unconsciously out of touch with reality.
So Pope, early in the poem, though he is out of harmony
with the world, is too complacently at home in that alienation.
He must move from this alienated distance through an
intense involvement to a final double vision that recognizes
a certain measure of alienation in the nature of things.
Unresisted alienation, like unresisted accommodation, reduces
experience to schematic abstraction and creates within the
self that life-denying condition that Pope recognizes about
him.

The question of alienation, then, in *To Burlington* as in the
other *Epistles to Several Persons* and the Horatian epistles, can
best be treated as a problem of knowledge, and three kinds of
knowledge are particularly important. At one extreme there
is schematic knowledge, which takes two forms, theodicean
and satiric. Both perceive pattern rather than presence,
substituting lucid and static schemes for the fullness of
experience. At the other extreme lies a third and more
mature kind of knowledge, the substantial knowledge that
we see in the closing vision of *To Burlington*. It is more
generous than satiric schematism but more tentative than

naive theodicy. It is a provisional kind of knowledge that grants the object integrity, even a certain measure of opacity, while trusting its own ability and need to know. The subject of such knowledge therefore inhabits a world that may, at any point, reduce itself to mere pattern or, like the Genius of the Place, suddenly meet the knower halfway in a moment of complex and substantial apprehension. Substantial knowledge permits the poet to enter a world that offers a certain existential fullness while retaining the poise of his self-awareness and individual integrity. His continual effort to achieve this knowledge and the world it discovers constitutes a central drama of Pope's poetry of the 1730s.

The substantial interpretation of experience that Pope achieves in *To Burlington* is embodied in the vision of useful art that closes the poem. It is a vision based upon a theodicean interpretation of the present and a hopeful projection into the future, and Pope acknowledges its precariousness. Yet it is not this poem's particular vision of useful art, or of the relationship between self and world, that will sustain Pope during the 1730s. It is rather the poem's structure of revision and self-qualification, its quest for the substantial knowledge that keeps alive the moral imagination. These poetic acts persist and constitute Pope's most authentic poetic identity. They will move closer and closer to the surface of his poetry as the figure of the poet moves closer to the center of its meaning. This pattern of "revision" also persists throughout the *Epistles to Several Persons* and the Horatian epistles. Its form is particularly clear in *To Burlington*, since the break is sharp (somewhat like the "turn" of an ode) and the poem is less progressive than suddenly self-qualifying. This "turn" becomes, in the later poems, distributed throughout the entire structure: sharp reversals give way to curves of increasing self-qualification, and sudden discoveries give way to progressive dramas of knowing. More and more, therefore, the crucial dimension of the poet's identity, and of his poems, becomes time, the vital and humanized time of poetic movement in which he discovers his world and himself, and in which moments of satiric and theodicean knowledge stand out like necessary — but necessarily temporary — islands in a moving stream.

iii. Myth, Money, and Negation: To Bathurst

> For my part I am grovelling upon this earth, and am contented with living in a state of indolence, doing a little good, and no mischief, to the best of my knowledge.... I am sure at this time I am a most innocent creature.
>   — Lord Bathurst to Pope, 9 Sept. 1732[20]

> Each good man trembles for himself in Balaam.
>   — Satire II.i. (Chauncy MS)[21]

Like To Burlington, the epistle To Bathurst exhorts the man it addresses to "proceed," to continue his exemplary activity:

> Oh teach us Bathurst! yet unspoil'd by wealth!
> That secret rare, between th'extremes to move
> Of mad Good-nature, and of mean Self-love.
>   (256-58)

Unlike the earlier poem, however, To Bathurst seems to present such activity as at best a stay against imminent chaos. In those few nobles like Bathurst and Oxford who remain virtuous, "English Bounty yet a-while may stand,/ And Honour linger ere it leaves the land" (247-48). Pope's theodicean perspective is thus sharply restricted. Of Timon's spending, he could say: "Yet hence the Poor are cloath'd, the Hungry fed" (To Burlington, 169). But To Bathurst presents the "balance of things" as an alternation of dehumanized extremes:

> Who sees pale Mammon pine amidst his store,
> Sees but a backward steward for the Poor;

This year a Reservoir, to keep and spare,
The next a Fountain, spouting thro' his Heir,
In lavish streams to quench a Country's thirst,
And men and dogs shall drink him 'till they burst.

(173-78)

Pope's appeal to Bathurst is therefore presented in the context of a vision of the world that seems to deny Bathurst significant influence. The poem offers no balancing theodicean perspective, yet it exhorts Bathurst in terms that became available to the poet, in *To Burlington*, only when such a perspective had allowed him to recover substantial knowledge.[22]

This apparent paradox can help us to see that Pope's deepest concern, in *To Bathurst*, is not with social change but with Bathurst's character: Pope attempts to bring about an intensification of Bathurst's virtuous activity. But this intensification depends on first winning Bathurst to a different way of knowing the world, a way that continually resists and complicates the schematic or mythmaking tendencies of the mind. Pope never quite says, and for good reasons, that one must learn to do without schemes and myths, but he does imply that there is more than a passing resemblance between mindless materialism and unexamined mythic or schematic thought. *To Bathurst* thus offers an implicit but powerful critique of the theodicean scheme that Pope had ventured near the conclusion of *To Burlington*. Yet it also strongly criticizes the purely satiric stance, which it identifies, even more strongly than *To Burlington* had, as the source of a life-denying mode of vision. This double criticism, and the absence of an explicit, substantial vision of experience, account for much of the difficulty and the power of *To Bathurst*, for they seem to deny the poem a fixed perspective, an interpretation of the world in which it can rest. But it is also part of Pope's argument that a fixed interpretation can foster a disastrous diminution of the self. To express such a belief without violating its spirit requires that it be dramatized rather than inertly stated.

We can best approach the meaning of *To Bathurst* by examining Pope's use of a few key terms. After presenting the fantastic vision vouchsafed by a wizard to "Much injured Blunt," Pope offers the following formulation:

> "The ruling Passion, be it what it will,
> "The ruling Passion conquers Reason still."
> Less mad the wildest whimsey we can frame,
> Than ev'n that Passion, if it has no Aim;
> For tho' such motives [*viz.,* those in 114-52]
>   Folly you may call,
> The Folly's greater to have none at all.
>
> (155-60)

Pope distinguishes passions, including the Ruling Passion, from motives. A "motive" implies intention, as in *To Cobham* where Pope speaks of those optimistic sages who would "Infer the *Motive* from the Deed, and show,/ That what we chanc'd was *what we meant to do*" (53-54, my emphasis). A motive is a passion transformed into intention by reason conscious of its aim.

The passions, *An Essay on Man* tells us, are "Modes of Self love" (II. 93), but what is the nature of a genuine aim? The aim of self-love per se is its own gratification, but it can hardly be correct to speak of the "aim" of so primary a force, and Pope never uses the word this way. Rather, in contrast to the centripetal energies of self-love, a true aim (and thus the possibility of a genuine act) requires a genuine perception of something outside the self. It is, moreover, upon this engagement and transformation of self-love by external reality that the creation of a true self largely depends. The discussion of gardening in *To Burlington* illustrates this idea. "Sense" is "A Light, which in yourself you must perceive," but which also permits you to glimpse "Nature," to "treat the Goddess like a modest fair" (45, 50-51). You must "Still follow Sense," but you must also "Consult the Genius of the Place in all" (65, 57). Only the man whose Sense permits him to see beyond his own ego and through the surfaces of nature will discover the Genius of the Place that will help to direct his Sense. If this is circular, it is a generous circularity that includes powers outside the self; it may remind us that genuine art is not the product of the isolated imagination.

Even the satiric figures in *To Burlington* operate within this scheme. Timon, for example, is not only a prodigal but a proud and pretentious man as well. His lavish expenditures are, transparently, means to all the wrong ends, but they are nevertheless means to an end. In *To Bathurst*, however, we are shown characters whose actions, though no less feverish than Timon's, are opaque rather than transparent precisely because means have replaced ends. These abusers of wealth are trapped in the thoughtless confusion of undirected passion. As Pope makes clear (109-52), one can only guess at their motives since they appear to have none, for the pursuit of means is the pursuit of the inchoate: "A feast is made for laughter, and wine maketh merry, but money answereth all things" (Eccles. 10:19). Since the self reflects its aims, and aims have been replaced by means, the self reflects the incoherence of means that have been directed to no end. The money-mad in *To Bathurst* display this incoherence; they are, almost to a man, self-defeating. Like Gage and Maria, they are "Congenial souls! whose life one Av'rice joins,/ And one fate buries in th'Asturian Mines" (133-34). As this example suggests, these individuals suffer a loss of friendship and genuine society as well: "to be just to these poor men of pelf,/ Each does but hate his Neighbour as himself" (109-10). Pope does not even allow them the community of thieves that Dryden's Shimei enjoys: "For *Shimei*, though not prodigal of pelf,/ Yet lov'd his wicked Neighbour as himself" (*Absalom and Achitophel*, 598-99).

The effect of wealth on individual identity is even more striking. Since the self-absorption that wealth fosters serves to destroy individuality, Pope's characters are continually dwindling to debased parodies of traditional roles. Cotta, who "was not void of wit or wealth," has just enough wit to rationalize his miserliness as a return to primitive asceticism: "If Cotta liv'd on pulse, it was no more/ Than Bramins, Saints, and Sages did before" (185-86). Cotta's son destroys his lands and wealth, and ultimately himself, in a career of prodigal "public service," a career (Pope implies) as remarkable for its misjudgment of the public rulers as for its debased notion of service:

> Yet no mean motive this profusion draws,
> His oxen perish in his country's cause;
> 'Tis GEORGE and LIBERTY that crowns the cup,
> And Zeal for that great House which eats him up.
> (205-8)

These roles are, at least in part, self-chosen. Other characters, however, suffer a replacement of the self by a series of externally conferred roles. We can still see the vestiges of mind and choice in Cotta, but the destiny of his son, by the end of his career, is merely a function of the roles conferred upon him by society. Were Cotta's son to be seen as a "Patriot," he would no doubt be rewarded; since he is seen as "the Bankrupt.... His thankless Country leaves him to her Laws" (217-18). Balaam's career is similarly a progress of roles and titles imposed on him by that meaninglessness which has replaced the moral will: Balaam, Sir Balaam, Director, and so forth. His wife's "Live like yourself" is perhaps the most ironic phrase in the portrait.[23]

Yet the effect of gold is to replace the self not merely by role or label but by sheer randomness. The limit approached more or less closely by all of the poem's wealth-abusers is the full loss of human status, the reduction of man to senseless thing. Pope's imagination of this condition is not as explicit as it is in *Epistle I.i.* where, "with the silent growth of ten per Cent,/ In Dirt and darkness hundreds stink content" (132-

33), but the possibility is continually suggested. If Hopkins'
tomb in one sense belies his life, in another it serves as a fit
emblem for it: "That live-long wig which Gorgon's self
might own,/ Eternal buckle takes in Parian stone" (295-96).
Or consider the portrait of Villiers:

> In the worst Inn's worst room, with mat half-hung,
> The floors of plaister, and the walls of dung,
> On once a flock-bed, but repair'd with straw,
> With tape-ty'd curtains, never meant to draw,
> The George and Garter dangling from that bed
> Where tawdry yellow strove with dirty red,
> Great Villiers lies . . . .
>
> (299-305)

The setting of past against present discloses, above all, the
loss of meaningfulness. Physical detail here gains its
significance chiefly from its having replaced the genuinely
significant. The George and Garter, as their place in the
catalog suggests, no longer function as operative symbols but
are as dehumanized as those impersonal, chromatic lovers,
Tawdry Yellow and Dirty Red. To describe Villiers, it is
sufficient to enumerate the things he has, in effect, become.

These examples suggest that *To Bathurst* treats moral
failure not simply in terms of pretense or affectation, as *To
Burlington* had done, but principally in terms of the traditional
Christian equation of evil with nonbeing, negation. Thus
Pope no longer displays the satiric certainty that appeared
in the earlier poem: "What brought Sir Visto's ill got wealth
to waste?/ Some Daemon Whisper'd, 'Visto! have a Taste,"
(*To Burlington*, 15-16). The "Daemon" was Pope's own
symbol for a want of realized character, and it is this baffling
formlessness that he confronts directly in *To Bathurst*. At the
same time, Pope introduces the Ruling Passion, which in
one sense "explains" the apparent chaos of much human
behavior but also acknowledges that the behavior, if the
character lacks an aim, may remain inscrutable.

Moral failure is nonbeing, but nature — even in the depraved world of *To Bathurst* — abhors a vacuum. As a result, means replace ends, roles replace selves, and the schemes of the mind replace the external world. Much of *To Bathurst* is an examination of such "pseudo-being," those substitutes for reality that only serve to separate the self from genuine experience. One of these substitutes is language. Pope at several points skeptically explores linguistic formulas, sometimes revealing the range of appetites actually implied by a seemingly bland phrase:

> What Nature wants (a phrase I much distrust)
> Extends to Luxury, extends to Lust:
> And if we count among the Needs of life
> Another's Toil, why not another's Wife?
>
> (25-28)

At other times, undercutting the pleasantly abstract with the more sinister concrete:

> Useful, I grant, it serves what life requires,
> But dreadful too, the dark Assassin hires:
> Trade it may help, Society extend;
> But lures the Pyrate, and corrupts the Friend.
>
> (29-32)

In the first passage, Pope restores the full range of reality implied by his terms, and he reminds us that the meaning of a term depends on its user. In the second passage, Pope does much the same thing for the concept of money. But the alternation of abstract and concrete instances in the second passage also carries the linguistic argument a step further. "Life" is not countered with "death," but with "the dark Assassin"; "Trade" is countered with "the Pyrate," and "Society" with the corrupted "Friend." Pope corrects the deceptiveness of linguistic abstractions like "life" and "Society" by uncovering the concrete. The lines are part of a persistent effort to restore to language — as to money and thought — its referential character, to replace the "pseudo-being" of mere terms or schemes or theories with the concreteness of substantial reality.

The same pattern appears in the larger structure of argument. By the close of the first section (1-80), much has been stripped away; the second part of the poem turns from the possible to the actual: "What Riches give us let us then enquire:/ Meat, Fire, and Cloaths. What more? Meat, Cloaths, and Fire" (81-82). Pope has not simply turned from one subject to another; he has also exchanged a speculative and fanciful mode of thought (the opening myths, the vision of "bulky bribes," the mock-hymn to "Blest paper-credit") for a factual survey of the fate of wealth. One reason for this movement from theory to fact becomes clear when we consider theories other than Pope's own:

> The grave Sir Gilbert holds it for a rule,
> That "every man in want is knave or fool:"
> "God cannot love (says Blunt, with tearless eyes)
> "The wretch he starves" — and piously denies:
> But the good Bishop, with a meeker air,
> Admits, and leaves them, Providence's care.
>
> (103-8)

Each man has an interpretation of the poor, and each interpretation serves to protect the self from reality, as from charity. Such "knowledge" is the epistemological counterpart of avarice, for just as money is significant only as it fulfills a purpose beyond itself, so knowledge ought to lead us out of our schemes and into the presence of what is to be known. Both avarice and schematic knowledge, however, avoid that conferring of significant purpose on means (money, intellectual schemes) by substantial contact with ends (good works, reality). Much of Pope's poetry is aimed at the intellectual errors propagated by immoral men, at the distortion of reality to suit merely personal ends. But much of his poetry is also concerned with the moral error propagated by faulty intellectual systems and inadequate modes of knowledge.

In *To Bathurst*, Pope attempts to redeem Bathurst — as he had redeemed himself in *To Burlington* — from this potentially disastrous mode of knowing the world about him. Indeed, the poem opens on a question of interpretation:

> Who shall decide, when Doctors disagree,
> And soundest Casuists doubt, like you and me?
> You hold the word, from Jove to Momus giv'n,
> That Man was made the standing jest of Heav'n;
> And Gold but sent to keep the fools in play,
> For some to heap, and some to throw away.
>   But I, who think more highly of our kind,
> (And surely, Heav'n and I are of a mind)
> Opine, that Nature, as in duty bound,
> Deep hid the shining mischief under ground:
> But when by Man's audacious labour won,
> Flam'd forth this rival to, its Sire, the Sun,
> Then careful Heav'n supply'd two sorts of Men,
> To squander these, and those to hide agen.
>
> (1-14)

Pope and Bathurst begin by confronting each other with rival views of wealth and of man cast into the form of myths of origin. The differences between these views are most telling. Bathurst is assured, even peremptory, and his myth is reductive, cynical, and deterministic. Pope is lighter, more tentative and self-mocking; where Bathurst "holds the word," Pope merely "opines." Pope's myth, in addition, grants man a larger measure of purposiveness and dignity, although his more complex view also suggests that man, and not "Heav'n" or "Nature," is responsible for human avarice.

More important, Pope manages to qualify the mythic mode itself. The smugly self-conscious parenthesis, the periphrastic niceties ("shining mischief"), the "heroic" diction and inversions (11-12), the very neatness of the account — these conspire to undercut myth by its own devices. Pope plays at mythmaking, but in the process he demonstrates considerable skepticism toward the entire enterprise for the same reason that he abandoned the Olympian stance in *To Burlington*: such knowledge separates one from the world of men and relieves one of human responsibilities. There is an unavoidable contradiction, for Pope, between membership in "our kind" and the sort of knowledge — schematic or mythic — that presumes to view man as wholly other, to be "of a mind" with "Heav'n." The human mind that claims such knowledge has always taken its own constructions for reality or ruthlessly abstracted a scheme from reality. In the process, it has pridefully, if unwittingly, isolated itself. The crucial difference, then, is that Bathurst's myth serves to separate him from those fools, men, while Pope's myth acknowledges his part in "our kind." Bathurst's stance is much like that of Pope at the beginning of *To Burlington*, whereas Pope strives for a way of knowing the world that will not undermine his ability to live in it, and with that ability his humanity. It is to such a mode of knowledge that he attempts to win Bathurst.

The same complex attitude, at once positive and skeptical, governs Pope's portrait of the Man of Ross:

> Who hung with woods yon mountain's sultry brow?
> From the dry rock who bade the waters flow? . . . .
> Whose Cause-way parts the vale with shady rows?
> Whose Seats the weary Traveller repose?
> Who taught that heav'n-directed spire to rise?
> The MAN of ROSS, each lisping babe replies.
>
> (253-54, 259-62)

The scope of his achievement, the atmosphere of *fiat* that pervades the portrait ("hung," Bade," and the like), the allusions to Christ and Moses present the Man of Ross "almost as a pastoral magician, whose intentions are realized by nature without the intervention of physical agency."[24] But the portrait is a curious mixture of pastoral and heroic

elements. Although Kyrle's success depends on the limited
scope of the community of Ross and its isolation from the
corruptness that plagues court and city, he nevertheless
bears a heroic burden of civic activity and becomes, in
Pope's account, almost a microcosm of the "well-mix'd state":
gardener, architect, doctor, lawyer, and benefactor. Pastoral
is traditionally an element of georgic, as of epic; but in this
instance it is as though Vergil's Corycian swain were not
simply contained within, but forced to reflect, the total civic
awareness of the *Georgics*. The resulting mixture of heroics
and excess, as readers since Johnson have noticed, creates a
significant tonal strain.[25]

If Pope, in this portrait, supplies "the final sanctions for
moral conduct," as Earl Wasserman has argued, his irony
also calls their finality — rather, his knowledge of their
finality — into considerable question.[26] The heroism of the
Man of Ross bears the same relation to the canons of realism
established by the poem as Pope's knowledge of "final
sanctions" bears to the possibilities of human knowledge
established by the poem. The latter are continually presented
as anything but final. This is clear in the opening exchange
of myths, and almost as clear in Pope's wry avoidance of
certain "final"questions:

> Say, for such worth are other worlds prepar'd?
> Or are they both, in this their own reward?
> A knotty point! to which we now proceed.
> But you are tir'd — I'll tell a tale. Agreed.
>
> (335-38)

Pope simultaneously affirms and denies the "truth" of the
portrait of the Man of Ross, as he does the "truth" of his own
introductory myth, because a moral goal that is both
attainable and fully satisfying — like a world perfectly
known — may imply a potentially disastrous imprisonment
in the static self. "There is no degree [of perfection]," writes
Pascal, "that is not evil if one halts there, and from which

one can keep from falling save by mounting higher."[27]

To claim, as Wasserman does, that "Bathurst must be won to the Christian life," and that the portrait of the Man of Ross "reaches out beyond human life, to the area of eternal life and the spiritual perfection it demands and justifies," is to miss the point of the portrait.[28] In neglecting the irony of this portrait, Wasserman also fails to see that Pope is not laboring to win Bathurst to a static goal, Christian or otherwise, but to a process, a continuous effort that will strive to surpass moral goals and intellectual formulations as soon as these are achieved. Human good, for Pope as for Aristotle, consists in "activity of soul in accordance with virtue," for "Strength of mind is Exercise, not Rest."[29] More strongly than *To Burlington*, *To Bathurst* thrusts the self into time and process. It is precisely the fictionality of the portrait of the Man of Ross that allows it provisional truth while encouraging the soul to continue its activity.

What is the nature of the activity to which Pope exhorts Bathurst? The portrait of the Man of Ross provides one kind of answer. In fact, it is slightly inaccurate to speak of a "portrait" precisely because the character of the Man of Ross is presented so thoroughly through his works. When Bathurst asks for details of his fortune, the question not only elicits an unexpected answer ("five hundred pounds a year") but in its insistence seems somehow inappropriate, almost a failure of decorum or understanding. Like his "real name," or his character apart from actions, Kyrle's fortune is less important than what it has been fashioned into. For the Man of Ross demonstrates that virtue consists in a full realization of the self through activity directed to an end. His example, however, cannot simply serve as a model of virtuous activity for others to follow. Bathurst's good works must differ from those of the Man of Ross because Bathurst is an aristocrat and because he is simply a different person.

Fully honoring these points, Pope delivers his principal exhortation to Bathurst in a highly abstract idiom:

> The Sense to value Riches, with the Art
> T'enjoy them, and the Virtue to impart,
> Not meanly, nor ambitiously pursu'd,
> Not sunk by sloth, nor rais'd by servitude;
> To balance Fortune by a just expence,
> Join with Oeconomy, Magnificence;
> With Splendor, Charity; with Plenty, Health;
> Oh teach us, BATHURST! yet unspoil'd by wealth!
> That secret rare, between th'extremes to move
> Of mad Good-nature, and of mean Self-love.
>
> (219-28)

Clearly, Pope does not outline a program of works for Bathurst as he had for Lord Burlington. The passage, especially in a poem that has persistently recalled us to the concrete, is a striking dance of abstractions and negative definitions that fairly cry out for concrete illustration, and this is part of its point. Pope can state abstractly what "we" need to be taught, just as he can express faith in Bathurst's virtue. But it is only the concrete act, luminous with animating intention, that can genuinely "teach us . . . That secret rare." Unembodied intention is, moreover, too much like those myths or rationalizations that permit others in the poem to keep their responsibility at a convenient distance. Thus Pope is asking Bathurst to objectify his virtue in works. "I will make living examples," Pope wrote of this poem to his friend Caryll, "which inforce best."[30] The moral satirist and the moral nobleman are governed by the same laws. Virtue is made visible and efficacious only as act.

There is another side to Pope's exhortation to Bathurst. Since riches are not in themselves expressive, their use will express the nature of the person using them; to suggest a program of specific benevolent acts is therefore to suggest a moral identity. In his use of dramatic audience, Pope, like Plato's Socrates, would rather create rhetorical conditions suitable to the choosing of an indentity than attempt to impose one from without. His exhortation to Bathurst, however, is also something of an example, and among its rhetorical conditions are two which at least suggest that Bathurst's future acts of benevolence will be less important than his creation of the very possibility of moral action in what had seemed an irredeemably paralyzing scene. There is the emotional acceleration produced by a heaping up of parallel constructions reinforced by enjambment (this is especially evident in 223-25). And there is the functional ambiguity of "Oh teach us, BATHURST! yet unspoil'd by wealth" (226), which seems at first only to conclude a lengthy period, but then also takes "That secret rare" for its object, thus initiating as well as concluding a sentence. These lend a strong measure of immediacy to Pope's speech, and immediacy of a particular kind. We hear a speaking voice that is not merely enunciating but discovering, building on its own utterance and expanding its vision of possible accomplishment. Unlike Bathurst's cynical myth, which sees human activity as a spectacle of mindless mechanism and separates a man from what he sees, Pope's exhortation enacts the free discovery and formulation of a possibility, and speaks not only for the poet but for "us" as well (226).

This seems to me the central significance of the exhortation: not its more or less adequate formulation of a golden mean, or its lack of "moral *Realpolitik*," as one critic has argued, but the exemplary act of moral imagination by which Pope, in appealing to Bathurst, frees himself from his earlier satiric and even mechanistic vision, and the greater freedom — evident in the very structure of the address — into which that initial act expands.[31] For Pope's epistle is not concerned with moral acts as such but with the conditions of their possibility. The chief significance of any act that Bathurst might perform will reside in the prior act of the moral imagination that will have created the possibility of virtue and freedom where none had previously existed. What Pope wishes Bathurst to do is, precisely, to discover what to do.

Bathurst's failure to perform such an act as Pope exhorts him to would deprive society of a much needed example, but it would also pose a threat to Bathurst's personal integrity. Along with Pope's gloomy remarks about the precarious state of English bounty and English honor in general (e.g., 245-48), there are sprinkled small hints that Bathurst's own virtue is not so secure as it might be. Pope addresses him as "yet unspoil'd by wealth" (226), and he speaks of "Your's, or OXFORD's better part" (243), referring no doubt to the contrast between these two virtuous noblemen and the corrupt majority, but perhaps also to the "better part" that Bathurst and Oxford, like most men, only sometimes play. Such instances of ambiguity require a context to give them point, and that context, in *To Bathurst*, is a pervasive atmosphere of moral decline. This is especially true of the second half of the poem, in which the number of "downfalls" narrated — Cotta, Cotta's son, Hopkins, Cutler, Villiers, and others — may at times lead us to suspect that we are reading a satiric adaptation of medieval tragedy.

The climax of this series of falls, and of the poem as a whole, is the tale of Sir Balaam, who is tempted, the narrator alleges, by the Devil. But the figure of the Devil, traditionally a tempter, is in this instance a fictional creation which the author of the poem "tempts" us to take seriously. At the same time, he warns us obliquely not to do so:

> Where London's column, pointing at the skies
> Like a tall bully, lifts the head, and lyes;
> There dwelt a Citizen of sober fame,
> A plain good man, and Balaam was his name.
>
> (339-42)

The column, as Pope's note informs us, bore an inscription "importing that city to have been burnt by the Papists," and it is thus a suitable emblem for the duplicity of the Londoners. But it is also a governing emblem of Pope's tale, a tale whose teller, like the authors of the monument's inscription, falsely imputes guilt to an external force, in this case, the Devil. Balaam cursing God, the Protestants accusing the Papists, Pope (as tale-teller) blaming the Devil — all are instances of the avoidance of moral responsibility by appeal to an external or nonexistent causal agent. The Devil in the tale is a final and climactic instance of "pseudo-being," the chief character in that mental drama that we stage to disguise and justify our own timidity, or ignorance, or corruptness.

The real "Devil" is Balaam's moral inertia, a failure to see and to will that results in the unconscious passivity brought out by the sexual aspects of the Danaë adaptation:

> The Tempter saw his time; the work he ply'd;
> Stocks and Subscriptions pour on ev'ry side,
> 'Till all the Daemon makes his full descent,
> In one abundant show'r of Cent. per Cent.,
> Sinks deep within him, and possesses whole,
> Then dubs Director, and secures his soul.
>
> (369-74)

Balaam is thus the climactic figure in Pope's presentation of moral evil as a negation of being, and the Devil is Pope's fiction to represent that negation. The pace of the tale, from the leisurely setting of the scene (339ff.) to the present-tense breathlessness of the closing lines (385-402), captures the acceleration of Balaam's fall into nonbeing, a fall occasioned initially by nothing more than moral inertia. And if Bathurst, witty pagan as he is presented to be, should discount the Devil for his own skeptical reasons, he can hardly fail to miss Pope's point. Like any reader of the tale, Bathurst must either agree that moral causality is the Devil's work or acknowledge that Balaam-like inertia is not neutral (simply a state in itself), but a failure of being that inevitably leads to evil because, as the abandonment of choice, it is itself evil. In Augustine's words: "The will does not fall 'into sin'; it falls 'sinfully.' Defects [privations] are not mere relations to natures that are evil; they are evil in themselves."[32] By the end of the poem, Bathurst must either accept the high moral task Pope has set, acknowledging the possibility of free action, or recognize the kinship of his stance with the complacent inertia of Balaam who, at first a "plain good man," finally "curses God and dies."

If the Devil is one kind of cautionary fiction, the *persona* Pope adopts to narrate his tale is another. His narrative stance, and the way of knowing the world that is implicit in that stance, significantly parallel Bathurst's stance in the opening lines of the poem.[33] Both Bathurst and Pope-as-tale-teller stand at a considerable distance from the world whose working they claim to describe. Both are privy to "Some Revelation hid from you and me" concerning the operation of that world. And in both cases, the burden of that revelation — man's predestination to folly; the malign efficacy of the Devil — is a denial of human freedom and responsibility. If Balaam's career projects in grotesque and exaggerated form the danger implicit in even a "virtuous" inertia, the narrator of that career interprets the world in a way that seems designed to foster just such inertia, and a version of just such a career.

The tale, moreover, as readers have often noticed, is something of a self-contained pendant to the poem, and when the poem itself ends with the tale we are made even more aware of its conspicuous irrelevance.[34] For the narrative of Balaam does not overtly acknowledge its connections with the larger context of which it is a part, nor does the teller acknowledge his connections either with the "Pope" of the body of the poem or with Lord Bathurst, who had earlier been a genuine presence in the epistle. Rather, the tale is offered as a *divertissement* ("But you are tir'd — I'll tell a tale."), and its content is treated as new information, presupposing no shared knowledge on the part of the dramatic audience. Balaam is placed at a much greater distance from Bathurst than are, say, the well-known Villiers or Cutler, and the tale-teller reinforces this distance with various "tale-telling" devices: the suspenseful increase in pace, the homely diction of the folktale ("My good old Lady catch'd a cold, and dy'd"), and the subordination of numerous potential complexities to the thrust of the narrative.

The effect of all this is to distance the tale from the dramatic audience in much the same way that Balaam's world is distanced from the tale-teller. To take the tale and its teller at face value is therefore to view them from the schematic perspective that the teller adopts toward Balaam's world, and which Bathurst had adopted earlier in the poem toward the world at large. To see through the tale and the teller, however, to acknowledge both surfaces and depths, is to understand them in a way that is analogous to the act of knowledge by which Pope, though not the tale-teller, understands the world. The audience who understands the Devil as a fiction masking nothing more than the moral inertia of Balaam also discovers the possibility of human freedom in a world, Balaam's world, that had seemed an inexorably determined causal structure as long as the Devil was taken seriously. To read the tale properly is also to know the world rightly.

Certain structural parallels between world and tale illustrate this relationship. Both, in their different ways, are relatively closed systems. Balaam dwells in a world in which events follow relentlessly upon each other, and in which the insistence of the pattern of demonic causality seems to squeeze out, so to speak, the possibility of human freedom. Even trivial or apparently irrelevant events are "ordain'd" by the Devil (383-84), whose causal web controls the world as completely as his influence possesses Balaam's soul (369-74). This appears most clearly in the description of Balaam's last days:

> My Lady falls to play; so bad her chance,
> He must repair it; takes a bribe from France;
> The House impeach him; Coningsby harangues;
> The Court forsake him, and Sir Balaam hangs.
>
> (395-98)

As these lines also illustrate, the tale itself displays what Joyce called a "goahead plot," a relentless linear thrust that is analogous to the causal insistence of the world it depicts.[35] When the beginnings of a digressive generalization do appear — "Things change their titles, as our manners turn" — the next line pulls us back to the narrative regardless of the violence done to rhyme: "His Compting-house employ'd the Sunday-morn" (379-80). The conclusion, similarly, distributes "rewards" with all the grim efficiency of a romance ending turned upside down:

> Wife, son, and daughter, Satan, are thy own,
> His Wealth, yet dearer, forfeit to the Crown:
> The Devil and the King divide the prize,
> And sad Sir Balaam curses God and dies.

(399-402)

The pattern of Balaam's world, then, in which the possibility of freedom lies latent in the midst of apparent determinism, is recapitulated by the very form of the tale itself. For to understand the world in this way is first to discover the possibility of another sort of meaning in a verbal structure that had seemed explicit and unequivocal. Pope does not merely present a moral or a meaning to Bathurst or advise him in the manner of "sage Cutler," "Live like me" (315-16). Indeed, it is precisely the latency of the tale's meaning that is its most significant feature. For Pope structures his climactic narrative in such a way that to understand it is to rehearse that difficult mode of knowledge with which Bathurst must come to view the world, a mode of knowledge that replaces the univocal constraints of mere scheme with the complex liberties of substantiality.

From the first, Bathurst is a figure whose way of knowing the world leads him to confront just such a closed system as Balaam's world and Pope's tale each constitute. Nevertheless, freedom must be found within the apparent mechanism of society; authentic meaning within the fantastic proliferation of tarnished meanings, theories, "revelations" and obsessions that the poem depicts; and a genuine self within the chaos of roles, compulsions, and false selves that make up the only world man has. How these are to be found is a secret known only to the moral imagination. That they may be found — that they must be found, or our humanity lost — Pope strives tirelessly to tell us. The humanity of the self is directly shaped by the possibilities for human freedom that it can discover or create in the world. In that creative discovery, the moral imagination finds the space of human freedom itself, and momentarily inhabits it.

The epistle *To Bathurst*, far more strongly than *To Burlington*, centers on the dangers to which the position of satiric adversary is prey. The satiric rigidity and the distance from the world that characterized Pope at the beginning of *To Burlington* are now assigned to Bathurst, while Pope devotes most of the poem, directly or indirectly, to winning Bathurst from that position. But Pope does not strive to win Bathurst to a specific position of his own, or to offer him a new interpretation of the world. Rather, Pope suggests that no real theodicean scheme is available to the man of honest perception, and yet that one's humanity cannot survive without the substantial knowledge that such a scheme can provide. This dilemma is resolved, insofar as it is capable of resolution, by the very doubleness, the self-qualifying and provisional nature, of substantial knowledge. The deadly absoluteness of both kinds of schematic knowledge, theodicean and satiric, paralyzes free and virtuous action in the world. It therefore becomes the task of the moral imagination to discover provisional rather than absolute truths, and opportunities for the exercise of one's humanity that will eventually cease to be fruitful, requiring new discoveries of the possibility of freedom. Thus, *To Bathurst* implicitly offers "definitions" of both knowledge and virtue as acts unfolding in time, acts requiring continually to be revised or made newly authentic. Moreover, the meaning of *To Bathurst* depends less on overt statement than on the significance of structure and style. The poem attempts to win Bathurst to a way of interpreting the world rather than to an interpretation, to a form of moral and cognitive activity rather than to an instance of that activity, and it does so by enacting rather than directly urging the poet's beliefs. In its aims and its methods, the poem respects both the notion of truth it has developed and the uniqueness of the man to whom it is addressed.

iv. The Road of Excess: To Cobham

New Hypothesis, That a prevailing passion in ye mind is brought with it into ye world, & continues till death.
— Spence's *Anecdotes*,
1-7 May 1730

It is the nature of an hypothesis, when once a man has conceived it, that it assimilates every thing to itself as proper nourishment; and, from the first moment of your begetting it, it generally grows the stronger by everything you see, hear, read, or understand. This is of great use.
— *Tristram Shandy*, 2. 19. 151

Taken in the order of their composition, the *Epistles to Several Persons* display several of the structural patterns that Maynard Mack has shown to be central to *An Essay on Man*.[36] The *Epistles* begin with a version of imperial myth and move along a curve of "constructive renunciation" that culminates in an affirmation of friendship, a "paradise" that is more inward and less grand than the vision of "Imperial Works," but also more human and sustaining. As in the *Essay*, moreover, two of the *Epistles* are devoted primarily to the qualification and casting away, and two to the revision and reconstruction of those schemes and myths by means of which the poet interprets and locates himself within the world. *To Bathurst* points up the inadequacy of such myths, but also affirms their provisional necessity. *To Cobham* ventures to construct not a new myth, but something more limited and theoretical: a view of human nature based on the hypothesis of the Ruling Passion.

This hypothesis in no sense supports a national or political myth reconciling the satirist with his world. Indeed, though *To Bathurst* is more savage and direct in its criticism of society, *To Cobham* takes social and political corruption even more thoroughly for granted, not so much treating it directly as referring to it incidentally as a well-known and scarcely alterable fact of life. While mocking the claim that character can be discovered by examining an individual's political or religious position, for example, Pope introduces the double-edged irony of this passage:

> Court-virtues bear, like Gems, the highest rate,
> Born where Heav'n's influence scarce can penetrate:
> In life's low vale, the soil the virtues like,
> They please as Beauties, here as Wonders strike.
> Tho' the same Sun with all-diffusive rays
> Blush in the Rose, and in the Diamond blaze,
> We prize the stronger effort of his pow'r,
> And justly set the Gem above the Flow'r.
>
> (93-100)

This is moral satire, but it is firmly located within a context of argument and intellectual satire, and it is subordinated to that main concern. This taking for granted of social corruption is matched by the attitude toward satire, for the satiric stance seems less an exceptional than a normative point of view. "The man to Books confin'd," for example, happens also to be a satirist "Who from his study rails at human kind" (1-2). Of the few virtuous characters in the poem, one "charms us with his spleen" (121), and another, "gen'rous Manly," raves at half mankind (116-17). Virtue and honesty, insofar as they make their way into the poem, rarely stray far from the splenetic. Nor do they make their way very far into the poem.

In addition to those few virtuous characters already mentioned, there is "gracious CHANDOS," who is "belov'd at sight" (113); there are perfunctory or ambiguous references to a few additional characters; and there is Lord Cobham who, if he is an "ideal figure," is so in a rather qualified way. The closing image of Cobham, of whom there are only a few images in the poem, is the following:

> And you! brave COBHAM, to the latest breath
> Shall feel your ruling passion strong in death:
> Such in those moments as in all the past,
> "Oh, save my Country, Heav'n!" shall be your last.
>
> (262-65)

There is dignity here, but the note of futility is also present. Cobham illustrates the persistence of a nobly directed Ruling Passion even to the moment of death; this is one reason for his placement in the gallery of humors that closes the poem. But his virtue is not elaborated, his political efficacy is not hinted, and his presence does little to revive the questions of social role and social possibility that *To Burlington* and *To Bathurst* had treated.

More thoroughly and explicitly than *To Burlington* or *To Bathurst*, *To Cobham* focuses on the theme of knowledge, and specifically, on the problem of acquiring knowledge of the characters of others. Cobham, we gather, distrusts book-philosophy, and assumes that knowledge can be rather easily acquired through observation. Pope, however, begins his own exposition with a warning against all extremes, and goes on to present, at considerable length, the perhaps unsuspected difficulties of the empirical method. Observation must deal with each man's distinctiveness ("that each from other differs, first confess"), and also his inconsistency ("Next, that he varies from himself no less"). If these arguments are extended to the observer, the results are even more discouraging:

> Yet more; the diff'rence is as great between
> The optics seeing, as the objects seen.
> All Manners take a tincture from our own,
> Or come discolour'd thro' our Passions shown.
> Or Fancy's beam enlarges, multiplies,
> Contracts, inverts, and gives ten thousand dyes.
>
> (23-28)

The a priori method faces comparable difficulties. The attempt to discover character from social position, education, or religion is crushed by the sheer weight of its own absurdities:

> 'Tis from high Life high Characters are drawn;
> A Saint in Crape is twice a Saint in Lawn;
> A Judge is just, a Chanc'lor juster still;
> A Gownman, learn'd; a Bishop, what you will;
> Wise, if a Minister; but, if a King,
> More wise, more learn'd, more just, more ev'rything.
>
> (87-92)

*   *   *   *

> 'Tis Education forms the common mind,
> Just as the Twig is bent, the Tree's inclin'd.
>
> (101-2)

*   *   *   *

> Is he a Churchman? then he's fond of pow'r:
> A Quaker? sly: A Presbyterian? sow'r:
> A smart Free-thinker? all things in an hour.
>
> (107-9)

In the first half of the poem, as these examples show, Pope considers and dismisses virtually every avenue to the knowledge of another's character. His earlier warning against extremes, from this perspective, begins to look like a denial of the very possibility of knowledge:

> And yet the fate of all extremes is such,
> Men may be read, as well as Books too much.

> To Observations which ourselves we make,
> We grow more partial for th' observer's sake;
> To written Wisdom, as another's, less:
> Maxims are drawn from Notions, these from Guess.
>
> (9-14)

The last lines of this passage suggest that the "fate" haunting
Pope's enquiry is not simply methodological: neither books
nor men, maxims nor observations, offer much hope for
knowledge.

Summarizing his skeptical survey with a sweeping series
of rejections (168-72) and a challenge to "Find, if you can, in
what you cannot change" (173), Pope himself "finds" it with
considerable abruptness:

> Search then the Ruling Passion: There, alone,
> The Wild are constant, and the Cunning known;
> The Fool consistent, and the False sincere;
> Priests, Princes, Women, no dissemblers here.
> This clue once found, unravels all the rest,
> The prospect clears, and Wharton stands confest.
>
> (174-79)

The Ruling Passion is not just "found" but invoked as well,
for it is neither an observable *datum* nor merely an
assumption. It is a hypothesis urging, first, that a search for
some sort of unity govern the examination of character, and
second, that this unity be sought at the level of the passions.
As a hypothesis, the Ruling Passion avoids the extremes
with which the poem opened; its validity, moreover, depends
not on a methodological preference but on the insight it is
able to supply. This is why Pope introduces the example of
Wharton so quickly, and why he chooses for his main
example a character of considerable historical immediacy,
reminding us at several points that he has done so: "Wharton,
the scorn and wonder of our days" (180). The structure of the
portrait of Wharton itself emphasizes this appeal to experience. It begins with the hypothesis: "Wharton . . . Whose

ruling Passion was the Lust of Praise"; goes on to interpret the data in the light of that hypothesis (181-205); and closes with, to say the least, a confident restatement of the hypothesis:

> Ask you why Wharton broke thro' ev'ry rule?
> 'Twas all for fear the Knaves should call him Fool.
>   Nature well known, no prodigies remain,
> Comets are regular, and Wharton plain.
>
> (206-9)

Neither Pope's exaggerated certainty nor his readiness to test hypothesis against experience should blind us to the imperfection of the method. Like any hypothesis, the Ruling Passion involves a certain amount of circularity. Against the overwhelming picture of flux and uncertainty that Pope offers in the first half of the poem, the Ruling Passion expresses an unwillingness to give up entirely the possibility of knowledge, an unwillingness to admit, as Henry Adams would admit, that "Chaos was the law of nature; Order was the dream of man," or that such order as (human) nature possesses is wholly undiscoverable.[37] The Ruling Passion does not imply that man is morally or rationally consistent, but that — at some level — the apparent chaos of his thoughts and actions is supported by a substratum of consistency. The hypothesis of the Ruling Passion is what keeps the question of human character, and of our knowledge of human character, from being merely an idle one. As Lord Bolingbroke wrote, "In all our attempts to account for the phenomena of nature, there will be something hypothetical necessarily included."[38] Like all useful hypotheses, that of the Ruling Passion occupies a fertile but uneasy middle state.

Pope points to this uneasiness in several ways, most obviously by means of an outrageous complacency. The lines previously quoted (206-9) do not simply restate the hypothesis, they also reduce Wharton — as the portrait had not — to a mere rule, an ostentatiously paradoxical epigram. The earlier "no dissemblers here" is similarly exceeded by the smug couplet on prodigies (208-9). This is Pope playing the role of the proud and overconfident investigator, as delighted with his own powers as he is with the results of his investigation. The lines on "second qualities" continue this role-playing in subtler ways:

> Yet, in this search, the wisest may mistake,
> If second qualities for first they take.
> When Catiline by rapine swell'd his store,
> When Caesar made a noble dame a whore,
> In this the Lust, in that the Avarice
> Were means, not ends; *Ambition* was the vice.
> That very Caesar, born in Scipio's days,
> Had *aim'd, like him,* by Chastity *at praise.*
> Lucullus, when Frugality *could charm,*
> Had roasted turnips in the Sabin farm.
>
> (210-19, my emphasis)

Like a Miltonic simile, the passage seems to develop according to some internal principle of growth. First, Pope flatly declares that Catiline and Caesar were driven by ambition. When he brings in Scipio, seemingly by the way, he brings in both an assumption — that Scipio, too, aimed at praise — and a slippery equation of Ambition with Lust of Praise.[39] At this point, it is not much of a surprise to discover that Lucullus also directed his efforts to what "could charm," for it has become clear that Pope is dramatizing the growth of hypothesis into axiom, that he has overgeneralized from the brilliantly successful instance of Wharton and grown "more partial for th' observer's sake." Pope nowhere says that such knowledge as the hypothesis of the Ruling Passion provides is provisional and imperfect, requiring always to be tested against experience, but he implies as much by dramatizing the reverse in a way that Sterne would have approved.

The rest of the poem extends this dramatization. From the

portrait of Wharton to the end of the poem, Pope's portraits become increasingly reductive and his hypothesis increasingly autonomous. The substantial complexity of Wharton is followed by the discussion of second causes, and this, after a brief transition (222-27), is followed by the seven humor characters — Cobham makes the eighth — with which the poem concludes. Indeed, the portraits are not just progressively reductive; they begin to be generated, rather than explained, by the Ruling Passion. The closing humors are illustrative presentations, brief and witty *exempla.* Pope ushers them in with an impresario's "Behold," and identifies them by type-names (Helluo) or characterizing phrases ("The frugal Crone," "The Courtier smooth"). These are literary characters personifying Ruling Passions, not human beings governed by them, and this portion of the poem, except for the incidental reference to Lanesborough, also moves away from the historically immediate and toward the ideal and typical. The Ruling Passion works best with a figure like Wharton, for his contemporaneity supplies a wealth of particulars that can convert schematic knowledge into substantial knowledge by checking the tendency of hypotheses to impose themselves upon the reality they are designed to interpret. The hypothesis begins to display that tendency when it is applied to figures who are considerably distanced by history, figures necessarily "literary" to the modern mind: Catiline, Caesar, Scipio, Lucullus. And with the closing humors, Pope seems to abjure, or no longer to need, the materials of history. Armed with the Ruling Passion, he travels the exemplary road of excess, the "high Priori road."

The self-consciousness of this strategy becomes still clearer when we consider Cobham's place in the conclusion. As the person to whom the epistle is addressed, he is in one sense the figure of greatest historical immediacy; yet he is reduced to a literary type of the patriot less complex than most of the humors that precede him. Pope allows the Ruling Passion to impose its greatest distortion of reality on Cobham, and he thereby ends the poem with a final *reductio ad absurdum* of his own theory. This is not to deny that the lines also manage to compliment Cobham, but merely to point out that the compliment only becomes acceptable when its reductiveness is understood to be self-conscious. In these final lines, Pope acknowledges the limits of his hypothesis, and he builds into that acknowledgment an indirect recognition of both the man behind the patriot humor and the poet and friend behind the single-minded theorist of character.

To Cobham dramatizes both the summoning up of the hypothesis of the Ruling Passion to deal with the apparent chaos of human character that is presented in the first half of the poem, and the gradual growth of that hypothesis, as it is applied to figures other than Wharton, from an explanatory construct into something like a constitutive principle. The idea of knowledge offered by the poem recognizes the crucial role played by the mind's constructive powers, but it also recognizes the tendency of those powers, when they are insufficiently checked by concrete reality, to distort that reality and at last to replace it with their own creations. The poem thus carries on the argument of *To Burlington* and *To Bathurst* concerning the dangers of reducing reality to a scheme or replacing it with an image. Its final reductiveness gestures toward the complexity it excludes, while the entire second half of the poem records the gradual entry of the poet into the community of fallible men that he had sought to explain by means of his magisterial hypothesis.

In the context of the *Epistles to Several Persons* as a whole, *To Cobham* is both a turning point, in its effort to create a unifying hypothesis, and a kind of rehearsal of themes, stances, and techniques that are more fully developed in *To a Lady*. The later poem, however, is more thoroughly personal, pays fuller tribute to the mystery at the heart of character, involves the poet in the fallibility of his subjects in more complex ways, and makes subtler use of the categories through which he tries to comprehend human character. In addition, *To a Lady* furthers the shift of emphasis from sudden reversal or epiphany to organic process that takes place in the course of the first three *Epistles*. In *To Cobham* a "privileged moment" of knowledge, the examination of Wharton, is followed by a series of validating errors or simplifications that qualify — but also authenticate — that moment. In *To a Lady*, as in *To Burlington*, the simplifications precede and are the condition of the moment of knowledge; but in the later poem, this "moment" is extended, and it is much less sharply distinguished from the process of exploration.

v. Satire, Tragedy, and Substantial Knowledge: **To a Lady**

> Woman and Fool are two hard things to hit,
> For true No-meaning puzzles more than Wit.
> — *To a Lady*, 113-14

> The truth is that he was during these years much thrown into the society of women, and thus came to sympathize with feminine sorrows.
> — George Sherburn[40]

To a Lady offers numerous instances of the forms of knowledge that appear in the three earlier epistles, and new relations among them. The satiric perception of mere pattern appears in the early sketches, and in portions of the later portraits as well: in the schematic changeability of Papillia, for example, or in the neat alternation of Locke and libido in Rufa. At the other extreme, substantial knowledge governs the poet's relationship to his Friend, a relationship of strong, sympathetic intimacy but also of mature detachment. Such substantial knowledge, a mixture of sympathy and distance, begins to enter the poem in the early portraits of Narcissa and Flavia, and achieves considerable power not only in the portrait of the Friend but also in that of Atossa. More than the other *Epistles to Several Persons*, *To a Lady* sustains, or continually renews, this difficult substantial mode of knowledge, not by rejecting the reductiveness of satire, but by accepting and humanizing it. Pope shows us that satiric schemes or categories, like any of the mind's structures, are always necessary and always in need of humanization. Without them, the mind confronts chaos; with them, the mind can permit itself to qualify and deepen the patterns they provide. If *To Cobham* shows that such structures can begin to dominate reality, *To a Lady* shows that they can also lead us to it.

In the early sections of the poem, as in the opening lines of the later portraits, the satire sharply polarizes subject and object, masculine poet and feminine victims. As the satiric inquiry deepens, however, the relationship between the poet and the women in his gallery becomes more complex. The detached exposure of a character composed of mere postures gives way to a more sympathetic and generalized concern with character itself: its tenuous coherence, its unpredictable energies and unsuspected depths. Pope allows us to see the connections between the grotesquely aberrant and the normal, between the stark contrarieties of a Flavia and the mere sequence of roles or attitudes into which anyone's continuity of self may, at times, break down. At such points, satire modulates to a near-tragic mode that presents the absurdities and contradictions of character with more pity and terror than ridicule. In this context, satiric irony is a way of approaching the challenging and mysterious, of mediating between the examining poet and his problematic victims until their separateness is partly dissolved in the sympathy of tragic knowledge and the shared burden of a common humanity.

We should, however, be wary of sentimentalizing the poem. Pope does not, in these portraits, simply abjure the sternness of moral satire in favor of a cozy recognition of the all-too-human. One of the most conspicuous strengths of *To a Lady* is precisely its ability to acknowledge the complexity and irrationality, the self-defeat and self-victimization exhibited by the various women, while still maintaining a firm hold on the moral sense and judgment that characterize Pope's satire. The poet may acknowledge that there is "a little Flavia in all of us," but he never forgets that there is considerably more in Flavia.

The tragic dimension of the poem is developed very gradually. In the opening portraits, Pope strikes quite a different note, drawing on the "gallery" tradition to provide a humorous and distanced tour of portraits that illustrate the casual remark the Lady "once let fall": "Most Women have no Characters at all" (1-2). The poet is at this point concerned only with postures, with the "Attitudes in which several ladies affected to be drawn"[41]. He further limits his examination by focusing on character only as it assumes certain extravagant and well-known masks:

> Let then the Fair one beautifully cry,
> In Magdalen's loose hair and lifted eye,
> Or drest in smiles of Sweet Cecilia shine,
> With simp'ring Angels, Palms, and Harps divine.
> (11-14)

The lady's very self-consciousness may lead us to infer a self behind these roles, yet Pope avoids treating character or motive at any significant level. His superior "Let" establishes the limited forms in which character is to be portrayed, and this tone of amused inquiry is fixed in the next couplet, which suggests such complete control over so trivial a subject that Pope can play at being a satirist: "Whether the Charmer sinner it, or saint it,/ If Folly grows romantic, I must paint it" (15-16). And despite a certain harsh intensity in the sketch of Sappho, the early portraits — Rufa, Sappho, Silia, and Papillia — are all clearly "literary" humors: trivial, emblematic, sharply limited, and greatly distanced from the poet.

Calypso, however, who follows these early sketches, is not quite so simple:

> Ladies, like variegated Tulips, show,
> 'Tis to their Changes half their charms we owe;
> Fine by defect, and delicately weak,
> Their happy Spots the nice admirer take.[42]
> 'Twas thus Calypso once *each heart alarm'd*,
> *Aw'd* without Virtue, without Beauty *charm'd*;
> Her Tongue *bewitch'd* as *odly* as her Eyes,
> Less Wit than Mimic, more a Wit than wise:
> *Strange graces* still, and *stranger flights* she had,
> Was just not ugly, and was just not mad;
> *Yet ne'er so sure our passion to create*
> *As when she touch'd the brink of all we hate.*
>
> (41-52; my emphasis)

The portrait says a good deal about Calypso's powers but strikingly little about her character. Pope draws on a vocabulary of demonic attractiveness to emphasize the powerful reactions she arouses, but there is an inexplicable conflict between cause and effect, character and response ("Aw'd without Virtue"). A footnote may explain this conflict by telling us that Calypso is "*Cunning* and *Artful*," but the portrait does not, and the "variegated Tulips" formula seems scarcely adequate to her powers. Yet Calypso does not so much outrun that formula as extend it, for her ability to charm us is also a comment on what we are able to be charmed by. If she was "ne'er so sure our passion to create,/ As when she touch'd the brink of all we hate," are "our" responses any more stable than her character, or any more our own than Calypso's mimicries are hers? The "nice admirer" who finds even her imperfections "happy" shows how an innocuous delight in the "delicately weak" can slide into an overrefined fascination with the perverse. In such an admirer we can discern the outlines of that later eighteenth-century figure, the worshiper of sublime powers verging on the demonic.

Pope, of course, calls Calypso "just not ugly" and "just not mad," rather than "sublime," nor is his rhetoric dissolved into rhapsody by her charms. There is an element of cool and powerful judgment in the portrait, the judgment of a mind that resists yielding to powers it can neither deny nor fully comprehend. The satire is deepened by the acknowledgment of a sympathetic response, while the response is contained within a moral judgment that saves it from sentimentality of either the benign or demonic variety. The response, however, is essential, for the portrait of Calypso is also, indirectly, a self-portrait, a record of the poet's reactions, not merely a distanced and impersonal sketch. The witty painter of feminine follies has begun to construct portraits of more complex women in which both subject and object, satirist and victim, play increasingly complex and interrelated roles. Pope's use of allusion reinforces this growing immediacy. Like Calypso (and Wharton, in *To Cobham*), a number of the women in the poem are referred to an "actual" past shared by the poet and, in some cases, by the Lady to whom the poem is addressed. This "historicity" (which has nothing to do with actual or supposed historical models) is especially important in the more elaborate portraits, which grant their subjects a more than literary reality and the poet a more than satiric degree of involvement.

Narcissa and Flavia take this involvement further, and begin to evoke the tragic sympathy that gives the account of Atossa much of its depth and power.[43] Both portraits fall into a three-part structure: a witty and distanced account of follies and contradictions; a brief questioning of motives; and a deeper vision of contradiction that sees inconsistency as self-defeat and particular faults as part of a shared heritage of human fallibility. After an initial account of

Narcissa's whimsy, Pope confronts the mystery of her character, the absurd way in which "whimsy" has deprived her of self-knowledge, community, and a stable identity. The questions that mark this deepened tone recognize her inconsistency as a form of habitual self-victimization:

> Why then declare Good-nature is her scorn,
> When 'tis by that alone she can be born?
> Why pique all mortals, yet affect a name?
> A fool to Pleasure, and a slave to Fame.
>
> (59-62)

As with Calypso, Pope seems to allude to the personal history of a woman "behind the poem," but at the same time, he generalizes that woman, moving from quirky particularities to encompassing universals, and from the idiosyncrasy of "And paid a Tradesman once to make him stare" to the generality of "A fool to Pleasure, and a slave to Fame" (56, 62). The oppositions in the third section of the portrait extend this movement: conscience and passion, atheism and religion, heathen carnality and Christian sobriety. The effect is to relate the turns and counterturns of mere whimsy to larger issues of conduct and belief, to connect Narcissa's idiosyncratic behavior with a more general human want of consistency, and to make of her, in a small way, an emblem of the unstable self faced with a life of moral choices.

Flavia, too, is at first brilliantly ludicrous: too witty for prayer, too romantic to envision death as anything but a stage triumph. But after Pope questions, "what can cause such impotence of mind?" (93), he moves into a series of paradoxes that replace the humorous irony of self-contradiction with the tragic irony of self-defeat:

> Wise Wretch! with Pleasures too refin'd to please,
> With too much Spirit to be e'er at ease,
> With too much Quickness ever to be taught,
> With too much Thinking to have common Thought:

Who purchase Pain with all that Joy can give,
And die of nothing but a Rage to live.

(95-100)

The generalized diction, as in the case of Narcissa, expands
Flavia's predicament into an illustration of the fundamental
opposition of character against itself. Unlike Narcissa,
however, Flavia is the first character whose acknowledged
wit and spirit lead to self-torment, the first instance of waste
and futility, seriously and sympathetically rendered. The
poet does not fully account for her; to grant her "Wit" does
not explain why the wit became an instrument of her self-
torment. Pope leaves us instead with an unanswered question
— "Say, what can cause such impotence of mind?" — and
with the unnerving and generalized spectacle of a "Rage to
live" that unwittingly but certainly courts defeat.

The character of Philomedé, added to the poem in 1744,
provides a necessary perspective on Narcissa and Flavia, and
on the direction of the poem as a whole.[44] At first, the sheer
blatancy of "Sin in State," the controlled satiric distance of
the portrait, seem merely a reversion to the earlier satiric
mode rather than a further development of Pope's more
substantial knowledge and sympathetic idiom. But this is
precisely what is required, for unlike Narcissa and Flavia,
Philomedé is in no sense her own victim:

> Chaste to her Husband, frank to all beside,
> A teeming Mistress, but a barren Bride.
> What then? Let Blood and Body bear the fault,
> Her Head's untouch'd, that noble Seat of Thought:
> Such this day's doctrine — in another fit
> She sins with Poets thro' pure love of Wit.
>
> (71-76)

Philomedé is not divided between her mind and her body;
the apparent inconsistency of her behavior masks a consistent
Ruling Passion.[45] Her pretensions are simply the servants of
her undiscriminating lust, and her head, if "untouch'd," is

also eminently tractable. Thus the second half of the portrait, the comparison with Helluo, does not expand Philomedé's behavior into an example of character opposing itself. Rather, it suggests that one pretentious vulgarian is much like another: "As Helluo.... So Philomedé." Philomedé is there to remind us that the increased sympathy of the portraits is not a sign of sentimentality, but of deepening perception.

The later portrait of Cloe functions in a related way. Like Fielding's Mrs. James, Cloe is a woman for whom "outward form and ceremony constituted the whole essence of friendship; who valued all her acquaintance alike, as each individual served equally to fill up a place in her visiting roll; and who, in reality, had not the least concern for the good qualities or well-being of any of them":[46]

> Would Cloe know if you're alive or dead?
> She bids her Footman put it in her head.
> Cloe is prudent — would you too be wise?
> Then never break your heart when Cloe dies.
>
> (177-80)

Cloe's inconsistencies, like those of Philomedé, are only apparent. Beneath the contrarieties of her behavior lies a self-absorption that is unswervingly consistent and unremittingly treacherous. Although Pope has gradually begun to construct his portraits from a perspective of greater involvement, his satiric distance in the Cloe portrait expresses the only "relationship" possible with a woman who lacks a heart, who "never, never, reach'd one gen'rous Thought," and who "cares not if a thousand are undone." The earlier mode is not merely revived, it is made fully functional.

In a different way, the brief sketches beginning with that of Simo's mate also allow us to see how far we have come.[47] At the heart of Pope's increased sympathy for the characters he examines is an increasing sense of their mystery and complexity. The questions Pope raised in the Narcissa and

Flavia portraits — "Why pique all mortals, yet affect a name?"; "Say what can cause such impotence of mind?" — are properly rhetorical questions, gesturing toward the lamentable capacity for self-defeat without claiming fully to comprehend it. Thus his admission, after the sketches of Simo's mate and the others, that "Woman and Fool are two hard things to hit,/ For true No-meaning puzzles more than Wit," may be set against a passage near the beginning of the poem:

> Come then, the colours and the ground prepare!
> Dip in the Rainbow, trick her off in Air,
> Chuse a firm Cloud, before it fall, and in it
> Catch, ere she change, the Cynthia of this minute.
>
> (17-20)

In this passage, women are difficult to paint only because they change roles so frequently. In the "true No-meaning" passage, however, figures who are scarcely more complex than those with which the poem began are called "hard things to hit" because they are genuinely puzzling. Like Philomedé and Cloe, Simo's mate and her sisters provide an essential perspective, a control. They show that it is not only the nature of the poet's subjects that is changing, but the very terms of his inquiry.[48]

With Atossa, we reach the poem's profoundest image of self-defeat and its closest approach to tragedy. "The forces at work within Atossa," Martin Price observes, "acquire more than human dimensions, and their magnification is insistently stressed."[49] Compare, for example, an early couplet on changeability with the opening lines of the Atossa portrait:

> How many pictures of one Nymph we view,
> All how unlike each other, all how true.
>
> (5-6)

* * * *

> But what are these to great Atossa's mind?
> Scarce once herself, by turns all womankind.
>
> (115-16)

Atossa's roles are the selves of lesser mortals. Although the "picture" metaphor in the earlier lines points to a reserve of self behind those roles, Atossa has no such reserve. Her stature derives in large part from her ability to *be* "by turns all Womankind" instead of merely affecting to be, and Pope mixes awe with satire from the very start. For Atossa is, as Price points out, "a near-tragic figure locked in a pattern of satiric transparency."[50] She "Shines, in exposing Knaves, and painting Fools,/ Yet is, whate'er she hates and ridicules" (119-20). She is drawn toward tragic stature by the thoroughness of her self-defeat and the energy and acuteness of her powers. But it is finally the capacity for self-knowledge implied by those powers, yet absent from her life, that shrouds Atossa in something like tragic mystery. It remains for the satirist, with considerable sympathy, to supply this awareness.

Much of Pope's sympathy is generated by his perception that Atossa, for all her singularity, is also a strongly representative figure, "an epitome of the inherent contradictions of woman," in Frank Brady's words.[51] This is emphasized not only by the range of Atossa's flights but also by the generality of the terms in which Pope describes her, and the similarity of these general terms to those which describe some earlier figures. The portrait of Flavia closes with these lines:

> Wise Wretch! with Pleasures too refin'd to please,
> With too much Spirit to be e'er at ease,
> With too much Quickness ever to be taught,
> With too much Thinking to have common Thought:
> Who purchase Pain with all that Joy can give,
> And die of nothing but a Rage to live.
>
> (95-100)

Here is Atossa:

> Strange! by the Means defeated of the Ends,
> By Spirit robb'd of Pow'r, by Warmth of Friends,
> By Wealth of Follow'rs! without one distress
> Sick of herself thro' very selfishness!
> Atossa, curs'd with ev'ry granted pray'r,
> Childless with all her Children, wants an Heir.
>
> (143-48)

Both of these passages combine respect for extraordinary powers with regret that they are wasted, that they contribute only to a pattern of self-defeat. Both passages also emphasize the clarity of that pattern, the unconscious reduction of life to the schematic barrenness of epigram: "Full sixty years the World has been her Trade,/ The wisest Fool much Time has ever made" (123-24).

Accompanying this clarity, however, is a deepening mystery suggested by the curious irony that the powers of an Atossa can utterly fail to constitute genuine character: this is the mystery of character itself. The full import of the poem's germinal remark — "Most Women have no Characters at all" — gradually begins to emerge. What had seemed merely glib generalization has grown into the perception that self-defeat, characterlessness, and squandered powers are more the rule than the exception. In recognizing that the grand powers of Atossa can result only in her defeat without a stable self to direct them, and in displaying a certain sympathy for this disordered state — generalized as it becomes in the course of the poem — Pope displays an awareness that the frantic and discordant in Atossa's nature speaks to us all.

Following the portrait of "a *Queen*," Pope invokes the distinction announced in the note to his first line and begins to consider the female sex "only as contradistinguished from the other." Again he begins with the schematic and reductive and gradually goes on to humanize them:

But grant, in Public Men sometimes are shown,
A Woman's seen in Private life alone:
Our bolder Talents in full light display'd,
Your Virtues open fairest in the shade.
Bred to disguise, in Public 'tis you hide;
There, none distinguish 'twixt your Shame or Pride,
Weakness or Delicacy; all so nice,
That each may seem a Virtue, or a Vice.

                                        (199-206)

For the first time, the poem looks beyond the behavior of
women to the social forces that in part dictate their coyness,
demanding certain patterns of behavior and imposing certain
roles. Women are "bred to disguise," "taught" the lesson
"still to please," and "curst" by "Man's oppression" (203, 211-
13). Thus, hidden connections lurk beneath ostensibly
parallel situations (and constructions): "Our bolder Talents
in full light display'd,/ Your Virtues open fairest in the
shade." The insecurities prompting purposely ambiguous
behavior and the social structures that shape feminine
conduct are shown to be the darker side of the categories so
readily assigned to the character of women. As Mrs. Oldfield
was to have said in Pope's Epilogue to *Jane Shore* (written in
1713), "Did not wicked custom so contrive,/ We'd be the best,
good-natur'd things alive" (13-14). Or as Pope had written a
few years before that in the "Epistle to Miss Blount, with the
Works of Voiture":

Too much *your Sex* is by their Forms confin'd,
Severe to all, but most to Womankind;
Custom, grown blind with Age, must be your Guide;
Your Pleasure is a Vice, but not your Pride;
By nature yielding, stubborn but for Fame;
Made Slaves by Honour, and made Fools by Shame.
                .   .   .   .

Still in constraint your suff'ring Sex remains,
Or bound in formal, or in real Chains.

                                  (31-36, 41-42)

Pope also allows the Ruling Passions of women a certain ambiguity:

> Those, only fix'd, they first or last obey,
> The Love of Pleasure, and the Love of Sway.
>   That, Nature gives; and where the lesson taught
> Is still to please, can Pleasure seem a fault?
> Experience, this: by Man's oppression curst,
> They seek the second not to lose the first.
>
> (209-14)

"The delicacy of the poet's address," observes Warburton, is apparent in his making this a "Pleasure of the *beneficent* and *communicative* kind, and not merely selfish."[52] But there is a more serious and less courtly dimension to this discussion of feminine Ruling Passions. Consider first the love of pleasure as Pope treats it in one passage from *An Essay on Man*:

> Self-love and Reason to one end aspire,
> Pain their aversion, pleasure their desire;
>
> .   .   .   .
>
> Pleasure, or wrong or rightly understood,
> Our greatest evil, or our greatest good.
>
> (II. 87-88, 91-92)

Pope argues here that the desire for pleasure is universal. Those men who "take to business" do so in pursuit of "pleasure" in its larger sense of fulfillment. When he assigns the love of pleasure to women in *To a Lady*, however, Pope is playing on the meanings of "pleasure." Denied a role in "business," and forced into the sort of decorative inanity that Pope had earlier satirized, women are able to find even limited fulfillment only in the pursuit of "pleasures," of those social vanities and *divertissements* that society has agreed are their proper province.

Love of "sway," similarly, is presented neither as a universal human goal nor a natural and God-given Ruling

Passion. For the denial of sway, of the independence and reasonable power that are naturally accorded by respect (the kind of frivolous denial Pope dramatizes *in propria persona* at the beginning of the poem), has raised the desire for sway to the status of a generically feminine Ruling Passion. The lines are no exoneration of feminine posturing but an admission that masculine society has made the disguise necessary and helped to dictate its forms. As Samuel Johnson said of the fate of women:

> However it has happened, the custom of the world seems to have been formed in a kind of conspiracy against them, though it does not appear but they had themselves an equal share in its establishment; and prescriptions which, by whomsoever they were begun, are now of long continuance, and by consequence of great authority, seem to have almost excluded them from content, in whatsoever condition they shall pass their lives.[53]

Such a view also governs the lines on "the fate of a whole Sex of Queens," which lament not simply woman but woman as she allows herself to be enslaved by the roles that are pressed upon her.

This generous and complex perspective expands still further when Pope announces, "See how the World its Veterans rewards!" (243). While the remark ostensibly refers to women, it embraces men and women alike, all who accept the forms and postures that offer themselves so readily but prevent the creation of a genuine self. At this point, in T. R. Edwards' words, "satire yields to something like a tragic view of the effects of time and change that everyone — women and men alike — must someday confront and yield to."[54] Yet the satire does not so much yield to as fuse with a tragic view. For if the poem laments the enslavement it depicts, it also affirms individual duty, the obligation to create a genuine identity from a chaos of impulses and appetites. Thus the closing address to the Friend is a recognition of rare fulfillment, a tribute to a woman whose freedom from pretense has made possible a genuine self and a genuine friendship, and who has miraculously harmonized those opposites that inhere in all character and could only fragment an Atossa:

> And yet, believe me, good as well as ill,
> Woman's at best a Contradiction still.
> Heav'n, when it strives to polish all it can
> Its last best work, but forms a softer Man;
> Picks from each sex, to make its Fav'rite blest,
> Your love of Pleasure, our desire of Rest,
> Blends, in exception to all gen'ral rules,
> Your Taste of Follies, with our Scorn of Fools,
> Reserve with Frankness, Art with Truth ally'd,
> Courage with Softness, Modesty with Pride,
> Fix'd Principles, with Fancy ever new;
> Shakes all together, and produces — You.
>
> (269-80)

The portrait of the Friend reflects the deepened conception of character acquired in the course of the poem. One critic has argued that "while Pope's objects of satire are present only as paintings, his Lady appears as a living being. The two-dimensional portraits therefore enhance one's sense of positive climax, because *it is only after passing over these dozen surfaces that we meet the rounded heroine.*"[55] But the description of the Friend, tender and admiring as it is, denies the entire procedure by categories on which it is founded and gives us very little "knowledge" of her character. To call the Friend a "rounded heroine" on the strength of a catalog of abstractions and generalities is to ignore the idea of knowledge that Pope weaves into his compliment. The poet's final tribute to his lady is his acknowledgment that she deserves all the labels of virtue and goodness that he heaps up, but that these labels in no way "explain" her or account for her achieved humanity. Unlike Atossa, the friend possesses a central self that is known through, but is not reducible to,

its attributes; Pope pays her the compliment of acknowledging, to borrow George Eliot's phrase, that "centre of self."
The self-mocking exhaustiveness of the catalog, the playfully
affectionate "receipt to make an Estimable Woman," and the
resulting "You" — these define Pope's affection for a woman
who makes a scant rather than a "rounded" appearance *in*
the poem, but whose character is affectionately acknowledged
by the poet's gesture toward the world behind the poem,
where there exists a woman whom he will not attempt to
"acount for" in his verse. This recognition of the limits of
poetic knowledge, and of the uniqueness of a genuine self,
honors the poet as well as the lady.

The portrait of the Friend thus brings to fulfillment the
progressive act of knowledge that is the central "plot" of the
poem. From restrictive categories of understanding, Pope
has moved to more generous ones, and from these, to a use of
categories that acknowledges their limits while gesturing
toward what they cannot capture. At the close of the poem,
Pope moves beyond even its primary category, feminine
character. It is this final movement that accounts for the
apparent defeminizing of the Friend in the "Contradiction"
passage that begins:

> And yet, believe me, good as well as ill,
> Woman's at best a Contradiction still.
> Heav'n, when it strives to polish all it can
> Its last best work, but forms a softer Man.
>
> (269-72)

The context of the passage is important. Pope has just
praised the Friend's equanimity ("Oh! blest with Temper,"
257-68), and now goes on to show that she nevertheless
transcends any simple idea of unity. His procedure is to
charge an idiom of polite male condescension with an
ambiguity that quite reverses the surface meaning. The crux
is "Man" (272). To read the passage as a "defeminizing," we
must take "Man" only as "male" and not as "human being."

But if we do take "man" as "human being," then "softer" becomes not a term of reservation but a compliment. In this light, the preceding couplet argues not that woman is, at best, merely "a Contradiction still," but that she is always, when at her best, not just an "unclouded ray" of Temper but a human being still. The passage asserts that the Friend, for all her equanimity, still participates in the rich and contradictory state of being human, that she has not bought unity with humanity. Pope depicts here a being who is freed not only from the psychic slavery of an Atossa or a Flavia but also from the rigidity of social and sexual roles and from the bland uniformity of a virtuous humor character. The passage alludes to the Friend's virtues but also to the mystery of the authentically human, which her virtue, like the poem, permits us to glimpse.

Pope's friendship with the Lady, and his participation through that friendship in a central or archetypal humanity, constitutes the reconciling myth with which *To a Lady* brings the *Epistles to Several Persons* to a close. It is both less and more than a national myth, such as *Windsor Forest* or even *To Burlington* offer, for its restriction of focus to the individual relationship expands, paradoxically, to embrace the more than individual and the more than national. The same pattern governs the process of knowledge dramatized by *To a Lady* itself, in which restrictive categories lead finally to substantial knowledge of the more than formulable.

This recovery of the human by means of a strenuous limiting of forms is a recovery for art as well, as we can see from Pope's changing attitude toward women as a subject for poetry. At first, women are mere decorative surfaces, "best distinguish'd by black, brown, or fair" (4), and the poet himself is merely a painter of "romantic" folly, trivially detailing the trivial:

> Come then, the colours and the ground prepare!
> Dip in the Rainbow, trick her off in Air,

> Chuse a firm Cloud, before it fall, and in it
> Catch, ere she change, the Cynthia of this minute.
>
> (17-20)

Somewhat later, women are more puzzling subjects, "hard things to hit" (113). Still later, Pope revives the early idiom of trivial virtuosity but now, largely through the ambiguity of "alone," he complicates it with the growing awareness of difficulty:

> Pictures like these, dear Madam, to design,
> Asks no firm hand, and no unerring line;
> Some wand'ring touch, or some reflected light,
> Some flying stroke *alone* can hit'em right:
> For how should equal Colours do the knack?
> Chameleons who can paint in white and black?
>
> (151-56, my emphasis)

After the ironic portrait of "a *Queen*," Pope effectively abandons the role of virtuoso and turns his attention to humbler subjects in whom the humanly significant is not overlaid with a tissue of glittering roles:

> That Robe of Quality so struts and swells,
> None see what Parts of Nature it conceals.
> Th' exactest traits of Body or of Mind,
> We owe to models of an humble kind.
>
> (189-92)

The turning away from "grand" subjects is still incomplete, however, for it is as yet *faute de mieux*: "If QUEENSBERRY to strip there's no compelling,/ 'Tis from a Handmaid we must take a Helen" (193-94). Only with the closing portrait of the Friend, in which, as Peter Dixon notes, "the operations of 'temper' and 'humour' assume something of heroic proportions," does Pope fully express the dignity latent in the subject he has been approaching.[56]

The imagery of this closing address, repeatedly stressing

the care of "Ascendant Phoebus" for a woman whose character has just been identified with "the Moon's more sober light" (254), points to that unexpected radiance of the voluntarily limited which is, in several respects, central to the meaning of the poem. In ascribing to this "gen'rous God" the Friend's possession of "Sense, Good-humour, *and a Poet*," Pope moves as far as it is possible to move from the virtuoso willfulness of the poem's opening lines, for he ascribes the rightness of his choice of poetic subject, along with the mystery of her character, to an artistry that transcends the personal.

It is not merely this ascription that convinces us, of course, but the development of the poem. We have seen that the poet earns the dignity of his subject in a sustained act of discovery, a sustained deepening of the forms of his knowledge. It is this that I would stress in turning from the *Epistles to Several Persons* to the *Imitations of Horace*. In the *Imitations*, Pope extends his recovery of the human from the materials of common life by focusing on the materials of the self. There, far more clearly than in the *Epistles to Several Persons*, the centrally human is glimpsed not merely in the self that is discovered but also in the self that strives to discover.

3 Scheme and Substance: The Epistolary Pattern

i. Introduction: Epistles and Satires

POPE'S first important imitation of Horace, *Satire II. i.*, was composed at the suggestion of Lord Bolingbroke. Describing the occasion for Joseph Spence in 1744, Pope recalled that Bolingbroke, in the course of a visit, "happened to take up a Horace that lay on the table, and in turning it over dipped on the First Satire of the Second Book. He observed how well that would hit my case, if I were to imitate it in English.... And this was the occasion of my imitating some other of the Satires and Epistles afterwards."[1] This nonchalant account may disappoint the reader who believes that Pope, with the *Imitations*, entered upon a significantly new phase of his career. The reader may suspect the poet of falling prey, in his last year, to the leveling powers of the "retrospective eye," or even of attempting to elicit from the appreciative Spence a remark like that which he placed after Pope's account in the *Anecdotes*: "To how casual a beginning are we obliged for the most delightful things in our language!"

Yet the casualness of the anecdote may serve to remind us of the connections of the *Imitations* with Pope's other poetry. In the two years following Bolingbroke's visit, and while he was at work on *An Essay on Man*, the *Epistles to Several Persons*, and *An Epistle to Dr. Arbuthnot*, Pope published two more imitations, *Satire II.ii.* and the unacknowledged *Sober Advice from Horace*. But Pope had been, as one of his editors remarks, "a translator and an imitator all his life," not just in his *Iliad* and *Odyssey*, or in the epic parody of *The Rape of the Lock*, or in the wide-ranging eclecticism of the *Essay on Criticism*, but in all of his major (and most of his minor) poetry.[2] We need only call to mind the Vergilian echoes at the close of the epistle *To Burlington*, or the free adaptation in the last paragraph of *An Essay on Man* of the Horatian motto affixed to the *Epistles to Several Persons* — or, more obliquely, the echoes in the *Imitations* themselves of Dryden's Juvenal and Persius, and Dryden's Lucretius — to appreciate that long before he undertook to imitate Horace, Pope had claimed the imitative mode as his natural poetic idiom. "Delightful *Abscourt*," he writes in *Epistle II.ii.* (significantly echoing Creech's translation), "if its Fields afford/Their Fruits to you, confesses you its Lord" (232-33). Something like this belief also governs Pope's attitude toward the fruits of other poets. As he wrote to his friend and mentor William Walsh: "A mutual commerce makes Poetry flourish."[3]

The *Imitations*, nevertheless, reflect thematic concerns that become particularly urgent in the period that began with the *Dunciad* of 1728 and ended in 1743. We need hardly consider Pope's abandoned plan for an *opus magnum*, a structure of ethic epistles introduced by *An Essay on Man*, to realize that the poems of this period represent different phases of Pope's effort to fashion a substantial interpretation of the world and of himself, an interpretation that would do justice to the difficult truth of each. For it is in relationship to the world that fulfillment must be found. Pope is not the poet of otherworldly solutions or flights into an escapist purity. Even the *Essay on Man*, for all its scope, insists as much as the *Epistles to Several Persons* or the *Imitations* that the "high priori road" is at all costs to be shunned, and that coherence of vision, if it is not to be merely hollow consolation, must finally fuse with the ignoble particulars of human experience. The varied tones of the *Imitations* — frustration, indignation, philosophic calm, playful self-mockery — acquire coherence once we see these poems as a dramatization of the quest for a substantial knowledge of world and self that is more discursively portrayed in *An Essay on Man*.

Yet the particulars of human experience, in the *Imitations,* seem more than usually ignoble. Pope never doubts for long that man finds "the private in the public good," but the service of the public good becomes increasingly identified with attack on public evil, or withdrawal from it. To seek fulfillment in the city, for example, is to risk losing oneself not in charity but in disintegration:

> Who there his Muse, or Self, or Soul attends?
> In Crouds and Courts, Law, Business, Feasts and Friends?
>
> .   .   .   .
>
> Shall I, in *London,* act this idle part?
> Composing Songs, for Fools to get by heart?
> > (*Epistle II.ii.* 90-91, 125-26)

One consequence of this bleak situation is that the circumscribed society of the poet and his friends acquires a certain symbolic depth, not simply because it is away from the city (this would be escapism) but because it fosters those social and cultural values to which court and city are inimical, because it mirrors in a reduced scale the ideal of an ordered republic, a harmonious society of shared values and individual liberties.

This combination of a restricted focus with a powerful texture of symbolic implication shaped the portrait of the poet's Friend at the close of *To a Lady,* and it shapes as well the features of the controlling symbol of the *Imitations*: the figure of the poet, the dramatized "Pope." Indeed, a major achievement of the *Imitations* is Pope's ability to treat the themes and problems of the *Essay on Man* and *Epistles to Several Persons* as problems of the self while still managing to invest them with a remarkable weight of implication and generality. There is a certain risk in making a major symbol of the self. In the satiric structure, for example, the knaves and fools are no longer contrasted simply with Lord Burlington or the Man of Ross, but with the poet as well. It is the poet who exhibits the self-awareness — at least — which all of his satiric figures lack. Yet Pope accepts that risk as inseparable from the moral authority he claims. And by communicating a powerful awareness of the recalcitrance of the self and the difficulties of self-knowledge, he manages, as T. R. Edwards says, "to keep the moralist's voice a human voice as well."[4]

This emphasis on the self controls both the thematic focus and the narrative modes of the *Imitations*. Here Pope fully exploits the self-dramatization and flexibility of the dramatic speaker that to a lesser degree mark the *Epistles to Several Persons*. The Horatian epistles, for example, most of which share the characteristic movement of the *Epistles to Several Persons* (from detachment to limited involvement, from schematic knowledge to substantial, and from the relatively fixed and static to the relatively open-ended and developing), thrust the poet much further into the foreground. He tries to discover how to live, and how to know himself. He is at times the object of his own approval and his own satire. He speaks in a range of voices whose breadth reflects his richly paradoxical nature. He discovers both his alienation from the world of men and women and his connections with it, and he frequently takes the very question of his relationship to the world as his explicit subject.

Satire and epistle are the two major genres of Pope's poems of the 1730s, shaping not only the *Epistles to Several Persons* and *An Essay on Man* but also the *Imitations of Horace, An Epistle to Dr. Arbuthnot*, and the *Epilogue to the Satires*. The structural pattern characteristic of each genre is determined, in Pope's case, by the acts of knowledge they dramatize and the aspect of the poet's identity they emphasize. In most of the satires (*Satire II.i., Satire II.ii., Epilogue to the Satires*), substantial knowledge and a substantial if uneasy accord with the world move inevitably toward schematic knowledge and radical isolation. In most of the epistles (*Epistle II.ii., Epistle I.vi., Epistle I.i*), the reverse occurs: schematic knowledge and extreme isolation are gradually replaced by substantial knowledge and a relationship to the world that combines both detachment and involvement. The pattern of the satires is thus basically tragic while that of the epistles is basically comic.

Another important difference between the satires and the epistles concerns the mode of the poet's relationship to the world. In the satires, where the poet is often engaged in dialogue with an adversary, the poem is itself a confrontation, dramatizing an immediate engagement of the world in an act of speech. It is this verbal immediacy, and the insistence of the adversary's aggressiveness or timidity or knavery, that raise the satire to the high pitch of denunciation characteristic of these poems. The poet's victims are correspondingly more evil than foolish. Their corruption is viewed not merely as a sign of weakness but as an encroaching threat to the decent man. The drama of the epistles, by contrast, is enacted not on the stage of public confrontation but in the hypothetical and contemplative space of the poet's consciousness. His relation to the world of folly and knavery is indirect. The satire therefore tends to be less vehement, and the victims tend to be more foolish than evil, cautionary examples rather than personal threats. The poet evokes them as symbols of self-defeat and then dismisses them, for they do not subvert the search for morality, but are simply inadequate to it. Since the victims are mainly their own tormentors, their activity moves closer to the pathetic or the tragic.

The satires and epistles also emphasize different aspects of the poet's character, partly by means of two different modes of self-presentation. Character, as Donald Cheney has remarked, may be conceived in two different ways, "as abstractly formulated datum and as dramatic quest." The heroes of Spenser's *Faerie Queene,* Cheney points out, "appear to be *embodiments of the virtues in their dealings with others* — showing the operation of Holiness or Justice on those who supplicate or challenge them — and at the same time they are *human figures struggling to realize their own identities in terms of these virtues.*"[5] In Pope's satires, the poet is above all an embodiment of virtue. He may display wit, pride, contempt, or naiveté, but he moves inevitably toward the sublime impersonality of Heroic Virtue, a human embodiment of the Good acting a part in the cosmic "Antipathy of Good to Bad." The mode of self-presentation in the satires is disclosure, the revelation of what is latent, and the plot of these poems is therefore more like a deductive sequence than an organic narrative. The latent forces in the poet's character are gradually made explicit as various figures and situations call forth his responses. In the epistles, the poet struggles to realize his identity in terms of those virtues that define his role as a satirist. He discusses himself, his aspirations, failings, inconsistencies, and accomplishments, and he enacts a drama of the personal effort to achieve a moral identity and a satisfactory interpretation of experience. The mode of self-presentation in the epistles is development, and their plot is one of organic movement and genuine discovery.

In each of these roles or stances, Pope achieves a certain symbolic power. The following examples are representative:

> O sacred Weapon! left for Truth's defence,
> Sole Dread of Folly, Vice, and Insolence!
> To all but Heav'n-directed hands deny'd,
> The Muse may give thee, but the Gods must guide.
> Rev'rent I touch thee! but with honest zeal;
> To rowze the Watchmen of the Publick Weal.
>   (*Epilogue to the Satires*, II. 212-17)

> But when no Prelate's Lawn with Hair-shirt lin'd,
> Is half so incoherent as my Mind,

When (each Opinion with the next at strife,
One ebb and flow of follies all my Life)
I plant, root up, I build, and then confound,
Turn round to square, and square again to round;
You never change one muscle of your face,
You think this Madness but a common case....

(Epistle I.i., 165-72)

In the first passage, from a satire, Pope is responding to the Friend's persistent reiteration of the question, "Where's th'Affront to you?" The Friend forces Pope to rise above the merely personal to a heroic assertion of the principle of Virtue. At this point, the poet ascribes the grandeur of his role to Virtue herself while he becomes a type of the virtuous man — heroic, vatic, emblematic — through whom the Good works its will. In the same fashion, the emblematic Triumph of Vice in "Dialogue II" of the *Epilogue* restates the relationship of satirist to society in the larger terms of the "strong Antipathy of Good to Bad." It is always the enormity of the vice confronting him that raises the poet to such virtuous and visionary heights. As particular knaves become transformed into details of a schematic Vision of Vice, the poet is enlisted in the "gen'rous Cause," at once depersonalized in the name of Virtue and individually heroic as the Last Just Man.

In the second passage, from an epistle, Pope himself displays the fallibility of his satiric victims, although he does so — as they do not — in full consciousness. At such moments, Pope moves toward a different kind of symbolic status. This self-portrait is the climax of a poem, which demonstrates (among other things) that the poet's inconsistency, his "Madness" as he calls it, is indeed "a common case," that all men are more or less unstable and self-contradictory. Against this background, his personal efforts to acquire coherence and integrity take on a more than personal significance. They become a particular instance of the perennial human effort to fashion a various and recalcitrant selfhood into an expression of an ideal of conduct, an effort whose rich literary tradition includes figures as different as Horace and St. Augustine, Montaigne and Benjamin Franklin. These distinctions between epistolary and satiric selves and modes of self-presentation are not absolute but matters of emphasis, yet the emphasis is clear and strong. Pope's whole poetic identity, however, must be sought in both kinds of poem, for each offers a characteristic kind of vision, stance, and act of mind that nevertheless constitutes only one side of that identity.

ii. The Epistolary Pattern: Epistle II. ii.

The *Second Epistle of the Second Book*, published in April 1737, was the first of the Horatian epistles to be imitated by Pope, although several satires had already appeared. Like the earliest of the satires, *Satire II.i*, the *Second Epistle* displays clearly the pattern of the genre to which it belongs. It dramatizes the poet's progress from solitude and detachment to a certain degree of involvement in the world; from inadequate formulaic images of self and world to a substantial knowledge of each; and from a grudging rejection of poetry to a recognition that the writing of poetry is both a necessary acknowledgment of his nature and a necessary engagement of the world. In an essay on Goethe, Ortega y Gasset says that the matter of greatest interest "is not the man's struggle with the world, with his external destiny, but his struggle with his vocation."[6] The remark might serve as an epigraph to *Epistle II.ii.*, for it defines one of the central conflicts of the poem. Pope's own Horatian epigraph — *Ludentis speciem dabit et torquebitur* ("He will wear the look of being at play, and yet be on the rack") — suggests the inwardness and intensity of that conflict. In Pope's case, the struggle with vocation is the most intense form of a larger and representative struggle with himself. The goal of this struggle, in

Epistle II.ii., is self-knowledge.

In the world of this poem, as in many of the *Imitations*, images of city and country define states of mind. The city is a place of distraction and chaos. Even if Pope, anxious to "smooth and harmonize" his mind rather than his verse, were to write again, "can *London* be the place?" The city fragments one's identity; it also holds more concrete dangers:

> A Hackney-Coach may chance to spoil a Thought,
> And then a nodding Beam, or Pig of Lead,
> God knows, may hurt the very ablest Head.
>
> (101-4)

Pope's hint for the pig of lead is a muddy sow in Horace, but Pope puts greater stress than Horace on the city's power to reduce men to the beasts they confront there:

> Have you not seen at Guild-hall's narrow Pass,
> Two Aldermen dispute it with an Ass?
> And Peers give way, exalted as they are,
> Ev'n to their own S-r-v — nce in a Carr?
> Go, lofty Poet! and in such a Croud,
> Sing thy sonorous Verse — but not aloud.
>
> (104-9)

The leveling "dispute" between man and beast, like the befoulment of the Peers, shows that the city is not merely distracting and unresponsive, resistant to the man as poet (as Pope's final cautionary remark suggests), but also positively inimical to the poet as man, dehumanizing.

The country, by contrast, is a place of "Ease and Silence," where "ev'ry Muse's Son" (even Blackmore) retreats to write verses. It is also a place that gives a man back to himself:

> Soon as I enter at my Country door,
> My Mind resumes the thread it dropt before;
> Thoughts, which at Hyde-Park-Corner I forgot,

Meet and rejoin me, in the pensive Grott.
There all alone, and Compliments apart,
I ask these sober questions of my Heart.

(206-11)

As these images of the self distinct from the mind, from
thoughts, and from the heart suggest, it is only in the
country and away from the "eternal roar" that one can
realize the degree to which he has become fragmented, his
humanity divided up among external claims. There is of
course no necessity in Pope's linking of rural nature with
moral integrity and self-knowledge. The country, as one
critic puts it, "is simply the place where virtue can be sure of
itself."[7] Indeed even this formulation may be too complacent.
Retirement can readily come to mean limitation, a naive and
untested state that has little to do with mature philosophic
simplicity:

The Man, who stretch'd in Isis' calm Retreat
To Book and Study gives sev'n years compleat,
See! strow'd with learned dust, his Night-cap on,
He walks, an Object new beneath the Sun!
The Boys flock round him, and the People stare:
So stiff, so mute! some Statue, you would swear,
Stept from its Pedestal to take the Air.

(116-22)

The "learned dust" and nightcap are Pope's addition. More
than Horace, Pope stresses the asocial privacy of the scholar,
whose mental life, like that of Johnson's astronomer in
Rasselas, has all the self-containment of fantasy.

The themes of fantasy and escape are central, and rural
retirement is only one of the forms in which they appear.
Survival in the city, for example, is "achieved" only by those
who manage to withdraw within it to a community of
illusion that sustains a common fantasy. The Brother Sergeants of the Temple, along with the role-playing city-poets

— "Let me be *Horace*, and be Ovid, you" (144) — who weave laurel crowns and frequent Merlin's Cave, demonstrate that the only city alternative to sheer fragmentation is a kind of parody-retirement. They surrender the fragile complexity of a true self for the more durable simplicity of entrenched delusion. Pope's notion, stated early in the poem, that he can separate himself from the world, that he is "indebted to no Prince or Peer alive" (69), and under no compulsion to write ("Sure I should want the Care of ten *Monroes*,/ If I would scribble rather than repose" [70-71]), is itself such a fantasy of escape.

In the world of *Epistle II.ii.*, however, the possibilities are very slim for a public role in which integrity can be maintained. "God send you well out of this World!" Pope once wrote to Mallet, " . . . . for to be well in it, you must be a Cibber."[8] The glancing allusion to Murray (132), who is mocked by the "Brother Sergeants," only serves to emphasize the plight of the upright public man. Yet Murray, if not "well" in the world, is nevertheless in it. He is not a Cibber, but neither is he "stretch'd in Isis' calm Retreat." And Pope himself, despite his concern to withdraw from the world, is also concerned, at last, to participate in it. For just as he believes that man finds the private good in the public, so he associates poetry with both philosophic retirement and "th'ambitious scene" of fame and public involvement. *Epistle II.ii.* is on one level an attempt to reconcile the impulse to poetic greatness with the quest for wisdom and self-knowledge, for a harmony of the inner life.

Early in the poem, there is a strong tendency to renounce poetry in favor of retired and philosophic leisure, and the poet's alternation between them is a sign of the degree to which he thinks them incompatible. Indeed, poetry and philosophic leisure do not simply alternate but burst in on each other. Pope's rejection of "scribbling" in favor of repose immediately precedes his lament: "This subtle Theef of Life, this paltry Time,/ What will it leave me, if it snatch my

Rhime?" (76-77). Pope's praise of "Ease and Silence," of grottoes and groves, is interrupted by the sudden and intense question: "How match the Bards whom none e'er match'd before?" (115). And his mockery of the city poets includes an acknowledgment of his own dealings with the Parnassian power structure:

> Much do I suffer, much, to keep in peace
> This jealous, waspish, wrong-head, rhiming Race;
> And much must flatter, if the Whim should bite
> To court applause by printing what I write.
>
>   (147-50)

This ambivalence finds a structural counterpart in Pope's movement from one verse paragraph to another. "The skillful handling of transitions," writes Reuben Brower, "for Pope as for Horace is not only a technique of style, but a technique of moving freely among moral and emotional possibilities."[9] Here, however, something like the reverse is true. The transitions seem to stand for the space between possibilities, the absence of a reconciling third term, and thus to make movement among such possibilities difficult rather than free. In the early part of the poem especially, as in one or two of Pope's other epistles, there is a more than Horatian abruptness about the transitions. This abruptness, a kind of reflective hiatus between paragraphs, is often found in poetry of an intense inwardness, which subordinates temporal structure to the reflective "now" of the speaker's consciousness (the transitions in Marvell's "The Garden" and *Upon Appleton House* are good examples of this). Pope's ambivalence is further brought out by his use of phrases that suggest a debate with himself ("But after all," "But grant"), and by the rhetorical questions that involve the Colonel, as a kind of sounding board, in the poet's efforts to argue himself into harmony. Here, as often in the poetry of the 1730s, the conversational rambling of the surface reflects the deeper interplay of warring impulses.

Such harmony as the poet achieves, as the relative violence of his psychic movements may suggest, resides as much in the conscious acceptance of duality and contradiction as in the unifying force of that "God of Nature" who is their ground of being (278-83). This harmony begins to take shape in Pope's picture of his own retirement. When he enters at his "Country door" (206ff.), he asks sober questions not about rural issues but about avarice, ambition, property, and hypocrisy. The country is used to gain perspective on precisely those aspects of the self that are associated with the vanity of the city, but which the immediacy and pressure of the city keep him from contemplating. The renunciation symbolized by withdrawal to the country now has nothing to do with mere escape, from either the venality of the city or from Pope's own involvement in it.

This simultaneous recognition of opposite impulses, this integration of areas of experience that were initially opposed, takes place on other levels as well: in the activity, for example, of "The Men who write such Verse as we can read" (158). Here, too, the passage opens with an emphasis on renunciation, on stripping away the tame or careless ("Such they'll degrade"); but it soon modulates to a description of bold and vigorous creation. Such poets will

> Mark where a bold expressive Phrase appears,
> Bright thro' the rubbish of some hundred years;
> Command old words that long have slept, to wake,
> Words, that wise *Bacon*, or brave *Raleigh* spake;
> Or bid the new be *English*, Ages hence,
> (For Use will father what's begot by Sense)
> Pour the full Tide of Eloquence along,
> Serenely pure, and yet divinely strong....
>
> (165-73)

The sense of freedom, of potency and vitality, is especially strong in Pope's verbs and metaphors. Just as his retirement from the city released the worldly wisdom of his heart, so the "severity" of the true poet liberates the resources of language. Nowhere in Pope does genuine renunciation mean impoverishment.

This pattern is enacted most comprehensively in Pope's discussion of property. All of the poem's partial vanities are caught up in the tyranny of possessions. To long for perpetual possession, to surround oneself with vast acres and splendid buildings, is to deny not only one's own mortality but also, in Aubrey Williams's words, the "melancholy pattern that nature itself must endure."[10] In the end,

> 'tis all a joke!
> Inexorable Death shall level all,
> And Trees, and Stones, and Farms, and Farmer fall.
> (261-63)

It is important to see that Pope is no more advocating a monastic frugality than he is a vain acquisitiveness. Each is not only an absurd extreme but also an imposition of an abstract idea of conduct on the needs of the self. What must dictate a man's use of externals is nothing less than his full identity, which differs from every other man's for reasons

> known alone to that Directing Pow'r,
> Who forms the Genius in the natal Hour;
> That God of Nature, who, within us still,
> Inclines our Action, not constrains our Will;
> Various of Temper, as of Face or Frame,
> Each Individual: His great End the same.
> (278-83)

Beginning with a discussion of wealth, the passage has risen to an entirely different plane of discourse. All questions of the use of things dissolve into the awareness that it is, above all, the self which we must learn to use and trust. For self-acceptance requires that we acknowledge the uneasy paradox hidden at the very center of our nature, and which we are always tempted to dissolve in the interests of a more stable, though limited and false, identity. Once the self is freed from those externals that obscure and fragment it, and from the sham simplicity of a vain inwardness, money — like poetry — can assume its rightful place as part of the expressive currency proper to human existence. It is a mark of Pope's increased awareness that poetry, which was earlier described as an "unweary'd Mill," is no longer an isolable talent but at one with the liberated self. More important, it is at one with the moral self.[11] The quest for self-knowledge is nothing more or less than a quest for that "God of Nature" which, once discovered and accepted, is indifferent to the particular forms through which the moral self is articulated. Like the Genius of the Place, it can be discovered only through a certain amount of intuition and persistent evocation, but when it appears it manifests a "rightness" to which the mind immediately responds:

> Yes, Sir, how small soever be my heap,
> A part I will enjoy, as well as keep.
> My heir may sigh, and think it want of Grace
> A man so poor wou'd live without a *Place*:
> But sure no Statute in his favour says,
> How free, or frugal, I shall pass my days:
> I, who at some times spend, at others spare,
> Divided between Carelesness and Care,
> 'Tis one thing madly to disperse my store,
> Another, not to heed to treasure more;
> Glad, like a Boy, to snatch the first good day,
> And pleas'd, if sordid Want be far away.

(284-95)

In his asides, which interrupt the flow of argument to dwell with quiet affection on his own idiosyncrasies, Pope brilliantly captures the accents of self-acceptance. And that acceptance includes the fertile contradictoriness of a complex identity: enjoy, keep; free, frugal; spend, spare; "Divided between Carelesness and Care."

Pope's poem is thus not only about the use of things but

about the full expression and liberation of the self through an act of knowledge. Property, patterns of experience, habits of mind, and imagination itself must be subordinated to the energies of "That God of Nature" rather than permitted to control them. Those external forces that cannot be tamed or escaped must be met with a voluntary response that transfigures their necessity. Just as Pope's father did not simply endure poverty with peace of mind, but "stuck to" it, so Pope's own attitude toward affliction and limitation shows that (as Williams puts it) "in the midst of loss, a dignity and a grace may be gained."[12] Pope discovers that such dignity and grace, in his own case, are achieved through the act of poetry. Johnson's words, in his *Life of Pope*, are particularly appropriate to *Epistle II.ii.:* "He considered poetry as the business of his life; and, however he might seem to lament his occupation, he followed it with constancy; to make verses was his first labour, and to mend them was his last."[13]

It is perhaps easier to say what Pope discovers in the course of *Epistle II.ii.* than to show how he manages to discover it. To attempt to chart the inner logic of the poem, the act of knowledge that shapes its structure and meaning, requires that we discover the poet's answers to questions that the poem raises only indirectly. How does one achieve self-knowledge? If the self can be changed, can it also initiate that change? Indeed, how are we to be made aware of the need for change, made to see that the tranquility we have taken for justified self-acceptance may be simply the specious comfort of a habitual role?

Pope deals with these questions of the progress of the self in terms of the dramatic movement of his poem. Its four fables in particular — the Frenchman and his boy, the soldier in Queen Anne's wars, the Brother Sergeants of the Temple, and the Lord *in primo Georgii* — bring to focus a structural point upon which the meaning of the poem turns: the relationship between the relatively fixed and static and the relatively changing and dynamic, between what we might loosely call image and process. On the most basic level, the fables provide illustrative parallels to the poet's largely autobiographical narrative. Yet like the tale of Sir Balaam, they are also striking examples of "conspicuous irrelevance." Like the extended similes of classical (as well as Spenserian and Miltonic) epic, the fables are invested with a degree of detail that calls attention to them as fables or images, as elements of the poem capable of being only imperfectly subsumed by the current of its narrative. Indeed, their very pastness lends them a certain detachability from the continuous present of the poem, and Pope (like Horace) places his fables before, rather than after, the incidents they are to illuminate, thereby leaving them momentarily pointless. Pope further accentuates the distinctness of the fables from the "main plot" by expanding Horace's self-conscious references to his fables and tale-telling — "castellum . . . . Nescio quid," for example, becomes "(Its Name I know not, and it's no great matter)" — or by introducing his own: "they record," "Don't you remember what Reply he gave?" (184, 49).

As a result of this use of fables, Pope's self-presentation, his progressive act of self-discovery, is dialectical rather than purely linear. The fables are invoked as formulaic approximations or models, and are then qualified and revised by the autobiographical narrative that follows them. The fable of the soldier, for example, ends with the soldier's refusal to fight when he no longer needs money: " 'D'ye think me, noble Gen'ral, such a Sot?/ Let him take Castles who has ne'er a Groat' " (50-51). Pope correspondingly says of himself:

> But (thanks to *Homer*) since I live and thrive,
> Indebted to no Prince or Peer alive,

> Sure I should want the Care of ten *Monroes,*
> If I would scribble, rather than repose.
>   (68-71)

Pope's assertion might conceivably be taken as a statement of independence that is compatible with the writing of genuine poetry, a rejection merely of "scribbling" (which suggests writing for hire).[14] It is quite clear, however, that for Pope at this point the rejection of scribbling means the rejection of all writing. The fable of the soldier has been taken to be a more accurate image of the poet than it in fact is. Thus, as though another side of the poet's consciousness were aroused by this misinterpretation of its nature, the lines immediately following are filled with a sense of loss at the anticipation of giving up writing:

> This subtle Theef of Life, this paltry Time,
> What will it leave me, if it snatch my Rhime?
> If ev'ry Wheel of that unweary'd Mill
> That turn'd ten thousand Verses, now stands still.
>   (76-79)

Only later does Pope fully recognize that to abjure Merlin's Cave is not to abjure poetry.

In one sense, of course, Pope recognizes this from the start. Yet much of *Epistle II.ii.*, and much of Pope's later poetry generally, is concerned with precisely this problem: our inability to "know," to take to heart and act upon, that which we know in a more superficial way. This pattern of delayed comprehension, in which the mind resists, or momentarily fails to absorb, or only incompletely absorbs the significance of the images it presents to itself, is the essential structure of the mental process that the poem dramatizes. Although Pope occasionally discerns this pattern in other characters ("And are you discontent/With Laws, to which you gave your own assent?" [29-30]), it is most tellingly dramatized in his own case. The movement of the poem could be described as the gradual "surfacing" of these implications until, immediately after the fable of the Lord, they are finally integrated into the poet's consciousness.

In the fable of the Lord, the self is at last invaded by forces outside it. More than Horace, Pope stresses the pressure of imminent awareness, the energy required to displace established patterns of thought, or stubborn illusions, or a recalcitrant will:

> There liv'd, *in primo Georgii* (they record)
> A worthy Member, no small Fool, a Lord;
> Who, tho' the House was up, delighted sate,
> Heard, noted, answer'd, as in full Debate:
>
> .   .   .   .
>
> Him, the damn'd Doctors and his Friends immur'd,
> They bled, they cupp'd, they purg'd; in short, they cur'd:
> Whereat the Gentleman began to stare —
> My Friends? he cry'd, p-x take you for your care!
> That from a Patriot of distinguished note,
> Have bled and purg'd me to a simple *Vote*.
>
> (184-87, 192-97)

Warton's comment on the passage is revealingly wrong-headed: "Much of the grace and propriety of this story of the Madman at Argos is lost, by transferring the scene from the theatre to the parliament-house, from poetry to politics."[15] But by eliminating the stage, with its irrelevantly complicating question of dramatic illusion, Pope has centered the fable squarely on the problem of delusions about the self, the conflict between reality and fantasy.

As this point, the self-reflexive aspect of the fables is clear. It is no mere convention of *style indirect libre* that sets Pope himself cursing "the damn'd Doctors" (192); like the Lord, Pope is reluctant to accept the lesson that forces itself upon him, and this reluctance is apparent even before the fable. His warm account of "the Men, who write such Verse as we can read," sealed as it is with a quotation from the *Essay on Criticism*, can only cast into doubt the honesty of the next lines:

> If such the Plague and pains to write by rule,
> Better (say I) be pleas'd, and play the fool;
> Call, if you will, bad Rhiming a disease,
> It gives men happiness, or leaves them ease.
>
> (180-83)

If "Plague and pains" is not an entirely candid and complete description of the poet's discipline, the "bad Rhiming" of *disease* with *ease* (which undercuts apparent meaning with etymological contradiction) assures us that our distress is to the point. These accents of resistance that precede the fable are matched by the grumbling notes (expanded from Horace's "nimirum") that linger on for a few lines after it:

> Well, on the whole, plain Prose must be my fate:
> Wisdom (curse on it) will come soon or late.
> There is a time when Poets will grow dull:
> I'll e'en leave Verses to the Boys at school.
>
> (198-201)

But from this point, Pope gradually moves to a larger synthesis of impulses and a fuller acceptance of self, not merely acknowledging but integrating those perceptions that he had previously kept at a distance.

The fable of the Lord, the three other fables, and the image of the retired poet that Pope offers early in the poem are all false or incomplete self-images with which the poet nevertheless finds it difficult to part. Indeed, the very suddenness with which Pope introduces the first fable seems to reveal a strategy of self-avoidance (3). The fables are not false only, for they eventually lead the poet to himself; but they are merely intermediate stages in the progressive act of self-knowledge that gives this epistle its distinctive shape and character. The fables are the schematic images by means of which the poet moves toward a substantial apprehension of his own nature. The absence of any fables after this, and of any further discussion of poetry, are signs that Pope is quite literally at one with himself. It is not simply a static image of the self that he comes to accept but also its process as well; and it is not a "poetic gift" but the "full Tide of Eloquence" that is one with, and expressive of, that process.

The movement through schematic images to a dynamic harmony takes a special form in the final passage of the poem when the Colonel tersely question: "But why all this of Av'rice? I have none." Pope responds in a vivid passage that is more than twice as long as its Horatian original:

> I wish you joy, Sir, of a Tyrant gone;
> But does no other lord it at this hour,
> As wild and mad? the Avarice of Pow'r?
> Does neither Rage inflame, nor Fear appall?
> Not the black Fear of Death, that saddens all?
> With Terrors round can Reason hold her throne,
> Despise the known, nor tremble at th'unknown?
> Survey both Worlds, intrepid and entire,
> In spight of Witches, Devils, Dreams, and Fire?
> Pleas'd to look forward, pleas'd to look behind,
> And count each Birth-day with a grateful mind?
> Has life no sourness, drawn so near its end?
> Can'st thou endure a Foe, forgive a Friend?
> Has Age but melted the rough parts away,
> As Winter-fruits grow mild e'er they decay?
> Or will you think, my Friend, your business done,
> When, of a hundred thorns, you pull out one?
>   (305-21)

Pope's catalog is not only longer than Horace's, it is also more extravagant and metaphoric. The proliferation of images, the sustained intensity of questioning that approaches pure interrogative energy, point to a deliberate attempt to strain the epistolary convention, to break down the distance between the Colonel (or the reader) and the poem in order to establish the kind of relation that finally exists between Pope and the fable of the Lord: a relation of moral immediacy rather than aesthetic distance. Pope's address must finally break in upon the Colonel as the fable of the

Lord broke in upon the poet himself, and the Lord's friends upon his fantasy.

The address, however, is not merely to be recognized by the Colonel as an accurate image of himself, for any image of oneself is a distortion of some kind. The address may nevertheless lead beyond itself to the activity of truth. Thus, Pope's speech is not an attempt to name the Colonel's vices; its very extravagance, its quality of trying to guess by naming everything, is a kind of admission that only the Colonel can truly know himself. Rather, Pope tries to initiate in the Colonel the sustained process of self-examination that the poem has dramatized, and that constitutes mature self-knowledge. Pope is acting the role of the Colonel's "own strict Judge" and intimating that the Colonel should himself do precisely that. The ending of the poem is therefore an exemplary beginning as well.

In the "Design" prefixed to *An Essay on Man,* Pope describes one of the merits of that poem as a "steering betwixt the extremes of doctrines *seemingly* opposite" (my emphasis); and in a number of the *Imitations of Horace,* as in *The Dunciad* and elsewhere, Pope demonstrates the tendency of two seemingly opposite forms of behavior to merge into equivalence. But genuine human existence demands not seeming but genuine opposites. It is not a bland harmony of ultimately equivalent forces but a tensional union of opposing impulses that we must strive to distinguish as well as unify. "This light and darkness in our chaos join'd,/ What shall divide?" asks Pope in the *Essay on Man,* and answers, "The God within the mind" (II. 203-4). The creative act of fashioning a self is here imaged as a process of separating and distinguishing, of dividing a uniform blur into clear and distinct forms. A number of Pope's later poems celebrate and dramatize such creative division, and *Epistle II.ii* is no

---

exception. Pope's closing exhortation to the Colonel, for example, is only one passage in which truth is approached through a kind of loyal opposition, an act of resistance that spurs examination and jostles old illusions. Another example appears in the poem's portrayal of false and true poets. Unlike "bad Rhimers," who "treat themselves with most profound respect," genuine poets are "Their own strict Judges, not a word they spare,/ That wants or Force, or Light, or Weight, or Care" (159-60).

Pope's approach to self-knowledge is also generated by opposition, by the moral equivalent of the writer's discipline. It is easy to forget that the poet, who ends by rousing the Colonel to philosophic activity, began by clinging to a retired scene from which the more public and involved Colonel (Cobham's and his country's friend) had already begun to prod him free by asking for verse. Throughout the poem, although Pope does not insist on this point, harmony threatens always to slide into static accord or bland unity, while opposition and tension — whether between a man and his work, or between one man and another, or between a man's image of himself and his real identity — liberate the energies of life and truth. Around the edges of Pope's fine portrait of self-acceptance and achieved harmony, in *Epistle II.ii*, these restless energies flicker.

iii. *The Excluded Middle Way:* Epistle. I.vi.

We can best approach Pope's version of the Horatian "Nil admirari" by looking at the closing lines of *Epistle II.ii*:

> Vivere si recte nescis, decede peritis.
> Lusisti satis, edisti satis, atque bibisti:
> Tempus abire tibi est: ne potum largius aequo
> Rideat, et pulset lasciva decentius aetas

("If you know not how to live aright, make way for

those who do. You have played enough, have eaten and
drunk enough. 'Tis time to quit the feast, lest, when
you have drunk too freely, youth mock and jostle you,
playing the wanton with better grace.")

*   *   *   *

Learn to live well, or fairly make your Will;
You've play'd, and lov'd, and eat, and drank your fill:
Walk sober off; before a sprightlier Age
Comes titt'ring on, and shoves you from the stage:
Leave such to trifle with more grace and ease,
Whom Folly pleases, and whose follies please.

(322-27)

Pope's admonition is more pessimistic than Horace's. Horace
assumes that some individuals know how to live properly
(*peritis*); to linger at the feast of life is therefore to usurp their
place. Pope is less certain that good men will take one's
place. By changing the metaphor to that of a stage on which
the vain actors of farce play to an equally shallow audience,
Pope sharpens Horace's argument from propriety into a
harsher reason for quitting the stage: in such a trifling scene,
the good man can only be out of place. The movement of
Epistle II.ii. from schematic images to substantial self-
knowledge, and from the poet's isolation to his qualified
reentry into the world, is complicated at the very last by a
paragraph which presents that world as a mere vision of
vanity.

This dark view is the rule rather than the exception in
Epistle I.vi., which was published nine months after *Epistle
II.ii.* The poem lacks the assurance of stance and vividness of
encounter that lend the satires their bold clarity, yet it is not
dramatic in quite the way that *Epistle II.ii.* and *Epistle I.i.* are
dramatic. *Epistle I.vi.* enacts the personal quest that characterizes the epistles, but arrives finally at the beginning, not
(as T. S. Eliot puts it) "to know the place for the first time,"
but to discover that it is no worse or better than any other
place. The poet's final acceptance of limitation, therefore, is
not an example of that internalization of necessity —

liberating and paradoxical — that we find elsewhere, but something more like wan resignation.

In the shadow of this pessimism, the folly of Pope's satiric victims acquires a new desperation; the fervency with which they unwittingly court defeat makes grotesque what might elsewhere have been comic. Timon, for example, is far more actively involved in his fate than is Horace's Lucullus. Timon's prodigal insouciance is a pose bought with shady persistence in corrupt measures that his lackeys carry out and he dare not acknowledge:

> A noble superfluity it craves,
> Not for your self, but for your Fools and Knaves;
> Something, which for your Honour they may cheat,
> And which it much becomes you to forget.
>
> (91-94)

These characters are no less trapped than those in other poems, they are simply trapped in more refined patterns. If Timon is conscious and cunning, there is nevertheless a level at which he is unaware of the bondage of corruption: "If Wealth alone then make and keep us blest,/ Still, still be getting, never, never rest" (95-96). The pursuit of pleasure also has degenerated to a hollow form that demands to be kept up yet paralyzes the responses it is designed to gratify:

> Go then, and if you can, admire the state
> Of beaming diamonds, and reflected plate:
> Procure a *Taste* to double the surprize,
> And gaze on Parian Charms with learned eyes:
> Be struck with bright Brocade, or Tyrian Dye,
> Our Birth-day Nobles splendid Livery.
>
> (28-33)

As Martin Price observes, "Pope beautifully catches the industry of enjoyment: the deliberate cultivation of fashionable tastes...the setting out to be 'struck.' "[16] Like the lust for power or money, the pursuit of pleasure ends as a form of imprisonment.

Indeed, nearly every activity that Pope describes ends in this way. The man who labors to win a wealthy wife also wins "such Friends — as cannot fail to last" (80). The man eager for "Pow'r and Place" laughs bitterly at the agents of official corruption upon whom his joyless success nevertheless depends. (107-9). Those who admire find that admiration must be paid out with the cheerless regularity of a tax: "Say with what eyes at Courts we ought to gaze,/ And pay the Great our homage of Amaze?" (16-17). Lord Russel, unlike Horace's Gargilius who comically purchases the object of his "hunt," is reduced to hunting a capacity for response, himself driven by his appetites:

> Up, up! cries Gluttony, 'tis break of day,
> Go drive the Deer, and drag the finny-prey;
> With hounds and horns go hunt an Appetite —
> So Russel did, but could not eat at night,
> Call'd happy Dog! the Beggar at his door,
> And envy'd Thirst and Hunger to the Poor.
>
> (112-17)

In the world of *Epistle I.vi.*, moreover, language itself may become a trap. The poem's first lines, rejecting the "flow'rs of speech" for the idiom of plain truth, are followed by a passage that deliberately flirts with the diction of sublimity only to repudiate it with the plain speech proper to the "philosophic" eye:

> This Vault of Air, this congregated Ball,
> Self-centered Sun, and Stars that rise and fall,
> There are, my Friend, whose philosophic eyes
> Look thro', and trust the Ruler with his Skies,
> To him commit the hour, the day, the year,
> And view this dreadful All without a fear.
>
> (5-10)

Pope elsewhere makes more satiric use of the elevated style. The precariousness of wealth, for example, is emphasized by the contrast between its unwieldy terms and the poet's more colloquial speech:

> Now, in such *exigencies* not to need,
> Upon my word, you must be rich indeed;
> A noble *superfluity* it craves,
> Not for your self, but for your Fools and Knaves.
>
> (89-92, my emphasis)

The language of Pope's own moral precepts even risks a certain plodding sameness in its concern to state genuine truths in genuine ways:

> If weak the pleasure that from these can spring,
> The fear to want them is as weak a thing:
> Whether we dread, or whether we desire,
> In either case, believe me, we admire;
> Whether we joy or grieve, the same the curse,
> Surpriz'd at better, or surpriz'd at worse.
>
> (18-23)

These character sketches and stylistic contrasts help to create an atmosphere of skepticism far darker than the mood of Horace's poem. It is an atmosphere in which the very possibility of meaningful action — or of discovering such action — is called into question, and it affects significantly the image of the poet. In the course of *Epistle I.vi.*, Pope moves from a position of real, if qualified, authority to one of utter uncertainty. This uncertainty is different from the easy tentativeness with which Horace ends his poem, and it is brought out in part by Pope's very reluctance to leave things as open-ended and inconclusive as Horace leaves them. Pope, for example, adds a climactic note to his penultimate paragraph by introducing it with the question, "Or shall we ev'ry Decency confound?" This sets off the final paragraph, with the advice of Rochester and Swift, from the preceding series of vanities, whereas Horace's remarks on love and laughter had simply continued that series. And

Pope reinforces the finality of this last paragraph with the introductory "after all":

> If, after all, we must with Wilmot own,
> The Cordial Drop of Life is Love alone,
> And Swift cry wisely, "Vive la Bagatelle!"
> The Man that loves and laughs, must sure do well.
>
> (126-29)

Horace, in short, groups love and laughter with the other vanities, but Pope attempts to treat them as final goods. Yet we are not convinced and neither is Pope. The line, "The Man that loves and laughs, must sure do well" is tellingly halfhearted. Its rhythm, its monosyllables, the pat flatness of its last phrase recall the emptiness with which Pope had described the final gift of wealth: "And then such Friends — as cannot fail to last." And in both cases, the anticlimax makes the caesura seem a failure of energy or belief rather than a pregnant pause.

Finally, Pope alters Horace's ending in such a way as to undercut further the authority of the poet and the certainty of his precepts:

> Vive, vale! si quid novisti rectius istis,
> Candidus imperti: si non, his utere mecum.

> ("Live long, farewell. If you know something better than these precepts, pass it on, my good fellow. If not, join me in following these.")

*   *   *   *

> Adieu — if this advice appear the worst,
> E'en take the Counsel which I gave you first:
> Or better Precepts if you can impart,
> Why do, I'll follow them with all my heart.
>
> (130-33)

By inverting Horace's lines, Pope ends with an appeal for better advice rather than a recommendation of his own, and he adds a deeply skeptical judgment of his concluding "love and laughter" statement: "if this advice appear *the worst*." The uncertainty of standards, the threat of moral confusion, are unmistakable. The confident teacher of the opening lines has dwindled to a confused pupil, and his unique formula "to make men happy, and to keep them so" — "Not to Admire" — appears at last to be just one more precept in a sea of directives to action. Like *Epistle II.ii.*, this poem begins with a schematic paradigm: not a fable, but a rule for approaching experience that will ensure one's happiness. Unlike the earlier poem, however, *Epistle I.vi.* does not move to a more substantial interpretation of experience but to a bleak perception of the relativity of all such rules, precepts, and paradigms.

Moral authority, however, is only one of the poem's major themes. An underlying problem is not that "nil admirari" is no better a precept than, say, "Get Mony, Mony still!/ And then let Virtue follow, if she will," but that it is no less a precept (*Epistle I.i.* 79-80). Pope's concern with language in *Epistle I.vi.*, his rejection of the elevated style in favor of plain speech and plain truth, conceals an opposition even more basic than that between true and false or forthright and ornate precepts: the opposition between the language of moral counsel and the realm of substantial experience. With the first line of the poem, Pope introduces not merely the question how to live but a miniature literary tradition addressing that question. " 'Not to Admire, is all the Art I know,' " he writes, " 'To make men happy, and to keep them so.' " Yet who is the "I" or these lines? It is, of course, Pope, the dramatic voice of the poem; but it is Pope speaking the words of Horace as translated (roughly) by Creech, Pope in quotation marks. The next lines insist on this literary lineage:

[Plain Truth, dear MURRAY, needs no flow'rs of speech,
So take it in the very words of *Creech.*]

(3-4)

It is odd to find such personal and individual counsel — "all
the Art I know...dear MURRAY" — appearing in so
thoroughly documented a form.

At one or two points in the body of the poem, Pope's series
of aphoristic couplets remind us that we are still in the realm
of moral discourse, thinking and talking about experience
(e.g., 18-27). But it is the closing lines that reveal most clearly
the distance separating this realm from that of firsthand,
substantial experience. Standing between Pope and a life
genuinely and properly lived are a series of authorities
(Wilmot, Swift), and their quotable precepts ("The Cordial
Drop of Life is Love alone," "Vive la Bagatelle!"), and even,
at the last, various names for the kind of advice they offer:
"advice," "Counsel," "Precepts" (130-32). This multiplication
of terms, with which Pope concludes the poem, is not merely
elegant variation; it is a reflection of the dead end in which
the poet finds himself, a dead end akin to that of the Prince
and Princess in Johnson's *Rasselas:* " 'It seems to me,' said
Imlac, 'that while you are making the choice of life, you
neglect to live.' "[17]

The language of moral discourse in *Epistle I.vi.*, like the
mythic speculation at the opening of *To Bathurst,* is only
incidentally a linguistic phenomenon. Its essential defining
characteristic, in the world of the poem, is that it is a form of
secondary experience, a form of activity that separates one
from full and substantial participation in the very experience
that is its central subject. It is this imprisonment in secondary
experience that accounts for the mode of the poem. Except
for parts of the brief address to Murray (38-53), *Epistle I.vi.* is
conducted in what might be called a pervasively hypothetical
mode. "If you believe X, then do Y" is the characteristic and
ironically applied formula of the poem, and one course of

action after another is entertained only to be dismissed. The poem offers us not experience, but various possibilities of experience. "But are thou one, whom new opinions sway, ... Fly then, on all the wings of wild desire!" (63-7). "Is Wealth thy passion? Hence! from Pole to Pole" (69). "If Wealth alone then make and keep us blest,/ Still, still be getting, never, never rest" (95-96). Even when the "If. . . . then" formula is applied to the best of choices, as in the closing lines of the poem, those choices remain hypothetical and secondary. It is not Murray or the poet — or even Wilmot or Swift — who act them out, but the hypothetical "Man" who has been, in one guise or another, the chief character of the poem: "The Man that loves and laughs, must sure do well."

As a result, the structure of the poem and the discourse of the poet are pervaded with a certain rootlessness, an inability to settle positively on a course of substantial experience, that is the grammatical counterpart of the insubstantial wandering and journeying (both literal and figurative) in which the poem's satirized figures are so frequently caught up. Indeed, in terms of the mode of his relationship to experience, Pope is curiously close to those characters who admire not real, beaming diamonds or real, reflecting plate, but "the *state* of beaming diamonds" and (worse yet) "[the state of] *reflected* plate" (28-29, my emphasis) The language of moral precept, the habits of the speculative imagination, and the categories of the skeptical intelligence seem to harden, in *Epistle I.vi.*, into a way of knowing the world that renders concrete experience of it inaccessible, and that thrusts Pope — although he is morally their polar opposite — into the very ontological limbo that imprisons the knaves and fools he satirizes.

The explanation of this meeting of opposites is only partly to be found in the form of the counsel "Not to Admire," in its status as counsel and thus as a mode of secondary experience. Its actual content is equally important. If those who are driven by admiration are enslaved, those who embrace the stoicism of the "philosophic eye" approach enslavement from the opposite direction. Even the tribute to Lord Cornbury, which one critic calls "the Epistle's most important positive statement," offers no image of positive action or belief.[18] Virtue, here, is renunciation:

> Would ye be blest? despise low Joys, low Gains;
> Disdain whatever Cornbury disdains;
> Be Virtuous, and be happy for your pains.
>
> (60-62)

To surrender oneself utterly to the world of appetite, avarice, and admiration; or to hover above that world, guided only by the negative counsel "Not to Admire" — these seeming opposites are merely alternative paths to the imprisonment of the self:

> Thus good, or bad, to one extreme betray
> Th'unbalanc'd Mind, and snatch the Man away.
>
> (24-25)

The Counsel "Not to Admire," of course, need not commit one to mere renunciation. Properly and generously understood, it is a kind of negative formulation of the doctrine of Use, urging not that we relinquish all worldly attachments, but that we avoid giving ourselves wholly to them. In this sense, "nil admirari" is, like Reason in *An Essay on Man*, "no guide, but still a guard" (II. 162), presupposing certain passions to be regulated and tempered. The middle way it implicitly recommends is not the deadly and programmatic moderation of one who is determined to care little about anything, but the more difficult and paradoxical "middle" that includes and miraculously harmonizes opposing impulses without first denaturing them.

In *Epistle I.vi,* however, "nil admirari" is understood in the simpler way, as a guide rather than a guard; the middle way for which the poet strives is not a harmonization but an

140 ACTS OF KNOWLEDGE

avoidance of extremes. As such, it has no substantial existence or positive nature, whence the unremittingly hypothetical mode of the poem and our sense that the poet is, finally, nowhere, that his espousal of the doctrine does not qualify and shape powerful and contradictory impulses but simply banishes them. The underlying problem is that the schematic paradigm with which Pope begins this poem is not, as in *Epistle II.ii.* or *Epistle I.i.*, an extreme state that must be qualified, but the very goal of such qualification. *Epistle I.vi.* is cast into limbo by its futile, direct pursuit of harmony that can only arise indirectly, from and through circumstances, from and through extremes. "Truth, being alive," as E. M. Forster has written, "was not halfway between anything. It was only to be found by continuous excursions into either realm, and *though proportion is the final secret, to espouse it at the outset is to ensure sterility.*"[19]

"Continuous exursions into either realm" are the temporal expression of a paradoxical nature; we cannot simultaneously pursue opposite goals. At the center of Pope's idea of human nature is no simple middle ground or third term but one of two things: either the miraculous nexus of paradox, harmonizing opposites without dissolving them, or mere nothingness. The first of these, and the center of a true self, we must actively create; since it is a tensional union of opposing impulses, we must distinguish these impulses before we strive to harmonize them. The second, the nothingness out of which we must create such an identity, is what we fall back into when we cease so to create. At these times, opposites are not raised above mere opposition to a paradoxical harmony but allowed to sink below it, to lapse into undifferentiated chaos and thus into equivalence. Then the difficult middle way that requires genuine opposites but is not reducible to them, the miraculous middle that constitutes a fully human identity, also ceases to exist.

iv. *The Limits of the Self:* Epistle I.i.

Pope's epistle to Lord Bolingbroke, in imitation of Horace's "To Maecenas," appeared in March 1738, two months after the publication of *Epistle I.vi.* and nearly a year after *Epistle II.ii.* It is the last sizable verse epistle that Pope would write, and it returns the poet directly to the problems of self-knowledge he had explored in *Epistle II.ii.* The epistle to Lord Bolingbroke is not simply a revival of that earlier poem, but something like a revision, for its movement toward self-acceptance is sharply qualified by the darker insights of *Epistle I.vi* into the poet's own limited nature and uncertain authority, his participation in the self-defeat and confusion that typify the world he satirizes. Thus, while *Epistle I.i.* exhibits the epistolary pattern of development from schematic to substantial knowledge, from isolation to limited involvement in the world, and from a desire for fixity to an acceptance of process, it seems also to strain that pattern and to present its alternatives in a stark and exaggerated form. The schematic paradigm with which the epistle begins is not a fable that we do not yet know how to interpret, nor an eminently plausible precept, but an image of the retired poet that is obviously partial, obviously incomplete. And the openness of its ending is so marked and seems to conclude so little, that one critic has called the poem "the most ambiguous and inconclusive of Pope's imitations."[20]

Between the schematic self-knowledge of the first lines of the poem and the inconclusiveness of its last lines, *Epistle I.i.* offers a vision of the world that is more distanced and unremittingly satiric, more schematic, than the visions of the world in the earlier epistles. The middle third of the poem is filled with images of mindless obsession and corruption, with individuals enslaved by passions they have long ceased to question or resist. In this world, one is "furious, envious, slothful, mad or drunk,/ Slave to a Wife or Vassal to a Punk"

(61-62). London's voice — "Get Mony, Mony still!" — and "the spectre of pale Poverty" relentlessly pursue the merchant to the earth's extremes:

> See him, with pains of body, pangs of soul,
> Burn through the Tropics, freeze beneath the Pole!
> (71-72)

"Spirit, sense, and truth" are no longer adequate virtues; "Honor" requires cash: "A pension, or such Harness for a slave/As Bug now has, and Dorimant would have" (87-88). The world is a scene of frantic acquisitiveness, where each man is both shackled and driven by his envy of another's wealth. Yet even "place and wealth" cannot bring enjoyment. The most one can hope for is to "have a Box where Eunuchs sing,/ And foremost in the Circle eye a King" (105-6). Here again, Pope adds a measure of debasement to Horace's victims. Horace's man of wealth is able to afford a seat at a bad play; in Pope, even the dubious appeal of the modish *castrati* is displaced by the desire to "eye a King." To be a courtier is to abandon substantial experience for the vacuous self-consciousness of courtly ritual. It is also to surrender integrity: "Adieu to Virtue if you're once a Slave:/ Send her to Court, you send her to her Grave" (118-19).

The common people are no better. "Alike in nothing but one Lust of Gold,/ Just half the land would buy, and half be sold" (124-25). Pope allows no qualification here and singles out no saving remnant as an exception to his schematic vision. This is a thoroughly demonic world, and when its "halves" are weighed in the balance, "neither side prevails,/ For nothing's left in either of the Scales."[21] The "mightier Misers" plunder their own country or, in a grander version of the merchant's feverish activity, sail across the sea to ruin foreign provinces. Of the less ambitious, "some farm the Poor-box, some the Pews." Still others pervert human relations to the ends of avarice, bribing "childless Dotards" with gifts of venison or wooing rich widows with "Chine and Brawn." Even the least ingenious have a part, for "with the silent growth of ten per Cent,/ In Dirt and darkness hundreds stink content" (132-33). With this funguslike accretion of interest, we can descend no further. The suggestion that money has usurped even man's modest organic dignity is barely countered by the final "content," which establishes that the "hundreds" are people rather then pounds sterling.

At this point, having risen to an intensity of attack that is characteristic of the satires, Pope turns from enslavement and makes its apparent opposite, inconsistency, his real target:

> Of all these ways, if each pursues his own,
> Satire be kind, and let the wretch alone.
> But show me one, who has it in his pow'r
> To act consistent with himself an hour.
>
> (134-37)

First there is Sir Job, whose whim to build on Greenwich Hill is almost magically converted into deed — and as quickly replaced by another whim:

> Now let some whimzy, or that Dev'l within
> Which guides all those who know not what they mean
> But give the Knight (or give his lady) spleen;
> "Away, away! take all your scaffolds down,
> "For Snug's the word: My dear! we'll live in Town."
>
> (143-47)

With Flavio and the uxorious fool, Pope's complication of Horace's view of character is clear. Horace's men simply praise the state opposite their own, but what are we to make of this?

> At am'rous Flavio is the Stocking thrown?
> That very night he longs to lye alone.

> The Fool whose Wife elopes some thrice a quarter,
> For matrimonial Solace dies a martyr.
>
> (148-51)

The sketch raises questions it cannot answer. Is Flavio's amorousness simply defensive bravado? Does the Fool think that he is happily married? Is he being faithful to the *idea* of marriage ("matrimonial Solace" does have a wonderfully theoretical ring)? Or is he simply too weak to do anything? Like characters in a bad play, these men simply do things for no reason. One can point to no specific disorder, only to the want of any recognizable order. These characters participate in the failure of mind that is portrayed most comprehensively in *The Dunciad*, for "that Dev'l within" is a version of Pope's powerful symbol of negation, the goddess Dulness.

The poor, equally inconsistent, mimic the mindlessness of the rich:

> They change their weekly Barber, weekly News,
> Prefer a new Japanner to their shoes,
> Discharge their Garrets, move their Beds, and run
> (They know not whither) in a Chaise and one;
> They hire their Sculler, and when once aboard,
> Grow sick, and damn the Climate — like a Lord.
>
> (155-60)

This portrait of the poor imitating the rich makes clear what has been less obviously true of inconsistency in all its other forms: its chaos is no less a kind of slavery than the persistent singleness of obsession. The world of *Epistle I.i.* illustrates more fully than any other of Pope's epistles the collapsing into each other of extremes that only seem to be opposites. It is a world of illusory extremes and ultimate sameness, a world lacking entirely those difficult and paradoxical modes of being which constitute, for Pope, the only authentic middle way because they do not shrink from, but incorporate, the energies of genuine opposites. The contrast between Pope and Horace is telling in this connection. Horace, through a series depending on *mutat*, emphasizes the number of objects that the poor change. Pope substitutes a dazzling string of verbs for Horace's *mutat*: the poor *change, prefer, discharge, move, run, hire, grow sick,* and *damn.* Pope's account, as a result, strikes us less with the variety of objects pursued by the poor than with their seemingly inexhaustible capacity to pursue. He takes us further "into" the activity, and closer to "that Dev'l within" the aimless. This movement inward to the very form of human aimlessness later permits Pope to implicate himself more readily in the prevalent inconsistency. Indeed, throughout the poem he transfers second-person examples to himself, aggravates Horace's account of his own failings, and insists that this mad inconsistency is indeed "a common case." The intensity of Pope's confession at the end of the poem, with its dissolving of the distance between self and world, is prepared for by this earlier movement toward an internal focus.

For much of the poem, of course, Pope stands at an immense distance from this world, viewing it as an ancient prophet might have viewed a city that was doomed to destruction for its evil ways. Indeed, his vision of the world is schematic to the point of being at times, even within the limits of the Horatian epistle, apocalyptic. There is the apocalyptic emphasis on utter moral clarity (here, absolute depravity), as well as an occasional image recalling the biblical Apocalypse:

> But show me one, who has it in his pow'r
> To act consistent with himself an hour.
>
> (136-37)

> Well, if a King's a Lion, at the least
> The People are a many-headed Beast:
> Can they direct what measures to pursue,
> Who know themselves so little what to do?
> Alike in nothing but one Lust of Gold,
> Just half the land would buy, and half be sold.
>
> (120-25)

There is also in the poem a version of the demonic causality that is characteristic of apocalyptic vision in the form (or nonform) of "that dev'l within/Which guides all those who know not what they mean" (143-44). Here, as in the early lines of *To Burlington*, the demonic vision is hardly to be taken with full seriousness; but it is not to be brushed aside either. The connections between Pope's way of seeing the world and the distancing and schematic clarity of apocalyptic vision are real and significant.

However distant from the world these motifs show Pope to be, he is nevertheless curiously close to it in another way, for the very pattern of extremes that underlies that world also shapes the course of his own development. *Epistle I.i.* revives the structural relationship between image and process that had controlled *Epistle II.ii.* and treats it both more minutely and more comprehensively. In this poem, Pope alternates sharply between poles of rigidity and flexibility, fixity and process, certainty and skepticism. On the level of language, this becomes an alternation between the concrete, public, and formulaic, and the abstract, private, and unformulable. Here again, the problem is to find a genuine middle way, for as Pope had said in the epistle *To Bathurst*, "what to shun will no great knowledge need,/ But what to follow is a task indeed" (201-2). At first, he is optimistic:

> Farewell then Verse, and Love, and ev'ry Toy,
> The rhymes and rattles of the Man or Boy:
> What right, what true, what fit, we justly call,
> Let this be all my care — for this is All:
> To lay this harvest up, and hoard with haste
> What ev'ry day will want, and most, the last.
>
> (17-22)

Dacier's remark on the Horatian original of these lines, "Voila une obéissance bien prompte" applies as well to Pope; there is a facile optimism about the lines, an almost performative assurance in the tone of the dedication to virtue.[22] The harvest metaphor, expanded from a hint in Horace, might be described (to adapt Whitehead's well-known phrase) as an example of the Fallacy of Premature Concreteness. The use of the physical analogy, with its seasonal security and definiteness, tells us less about the real nature of Pope's task than about the strength of his will to accomplish it and the degree to which he sees it, at this point, in terms of its ultimate accomplishment. Pope imagines his task to be single and finite, something to be completed once for all, just as he imagines a last day that is more important than the overall process of a life in which each day — first, last, or intermediate — is only an artificially isolated moment (22).

The inadequacy of this view becomes clear in the lines that follow. Their freedom and diversity imply a view of character with which Pope's resolutions scarcely begin to come to terms:

> But ask not, to what Doctors I apply?
> Sworn to no Master, of no Sect am I:
> As drives the storm, at any door I knock,
> And house with Montagne now, or now with Lock.
> Sometimes a Patriot, active in debate,
> Mix with the World, and battle for the State,
> Free as young Lyttleton, her cause pursue,
> Still true to Virtue, and as warm as true:
> Sometimes, with Aristippus, or St. Paul,
> Indulge my Candor, and grow all to all;
> Back to my native Moderation slide,
> And win my way by yielding to the tyde.
>
> (23-34)

Reuben Brower objects that Pope does not take us so deeply as Horace into the philosophical positions he mentions, but this seems precisely the point.[23] Such beautifully generalized lines as "Mix with the World, and battle for the State" point not to a submersion of self in doctrine or sect but to those energies that use St. Paul or Aristippus without a surrender of identity. In such a passage, the richness and possibility — as well as some of the effortlessness — of the comic vision momentarily displace the single-minded responsibility of the moralist's more austere attitude. It is a humanizing interlude, but it forces a revision of Pope's task. Harvesting and hoarding are no longer adequate metaphors for the process by which virtue and coherence can be established in the vital self that has just voiced its complex freedom. Thus, Pope next describes at length how

> slow th'unprofitable Moments roll,
> That lock up all the Functions of my soul;
> That keep me from Myself; and still delay
> Life's instant business to a future day.
>
> (39-42)

We have now come a certain distance. Virtue is no longer an external substance to be hoarded against the spiritual needs of the last day; rather, it is bound up with the activity of attending to the self, and, more important, with a freeing of "the Functions of my soul." This image does more justice than the harvest metaphor to the vitality of the *nullius in verba* passage, and recalls the liberation that is made possible by frugality, by the rules of poetry, and by a persistent self-examination in *Epistle II.ii.*

Like *Epistle II.ii.*, then, this portion of the poem proceeds dialectically. In the next paragraph (47-54), Pope speaks of putting himself to school, and here again — in the references to his physical weakness, and in his refashioning of Horace's abstract observation, "Est quadam prodire tenus, si non datur ultra," into an image of walking and dancing — he enjoys a certain optimistic concreteness that an abstract discourse could not support. Moreover, the remark that "men must walk at least before they dance," though it connects a project of moral effort with concrete, physical activity, connects it as well — at least by suggestion — with an inevitable and effortless process of physical maturation.

This prepares for the surprising lines that follow:

> Say, does thy blood rebel, thy bosom move
> With wretched Av'rice, or as wretched Love?
> Know, there are Words, and Spells, which can controll
> (Between the Fits) this Fever of the soul:
> Know, there are Rhymes, which (fresh and fresh apply'd)
> Will cure the arrant'st Puppy of his Pride.
> Be furious, envious, slothful, mad or drunk,
> Slave to a Wife or Vassal to a Punk,
> A Switz, a High-dutch, or a Low-dutch Bear —
> All that we ask is but a patient Ear.
>
> (55-64)

The bold certainty of this dedication clearly extends the deceptive physical analogies of the preceding lines. The problem of acquiring virtue has been simplified to the more modest problem of curing specific vices, and these vices are imaged as mere physical infirmities.

Yet the whole self resists such simplification even as it seeks it. Pope's parenthetical remarks in this passage are more skeptical than Horace's; their very placement mimics a reluctance to claim as much as is claimed by the ends of the clauses they interrupt. And the momentous tone of the passage, its strain and bravado — the final line sounds like an advertisement for Ward's Drop — undercuts such optimism in the very act of expressing it. This pattern of simplified assertion and complicating qualification has, in fact, dominated the poem up to this point. The verse paragraphs beginning at lines 17, 35, 47 and 55 all move from preliminary bluster and optimistic resolve to more qualified, difficult, and subtle assertions, suggesting that such bluster and resolve can be a means to self-avoidance as easily as to self-confrontation (just as precepts, in *Epistle I.vi.*, isolated the poet from the experience they were to have organized and made available). The theme of self-avoidance is still clearer when, after these preparations, Pope turns not to himself but to the world (55), having changed the subject of the preceding lines from Horace's "you" to "I" in order to emphasize just this contrast (49-54).

The concrete images, the formulaic pronouncements and resolves, the cures and "receipts to make a virtuous soul" — all prove, at last, to depend on too simple an idea of virtue and too simple an idea of the self. Yet the opposite extreme holds comparable dangers. If virtue is not something to be hoarded, and the "Fever of the soul" is not to be cured by words and spells, some of the matter-of-fact concreteness of such images may nevertheless enter into more complex and adequate formulations. If it does not, then one extreme will merely be replaced by another. The chief characteristic of the self may then come to be its protean shapelessness, and the chief characteristic of virtue its inwardness and ineffability. The only acceptable condition of soul, in such a case, is a purity untarnished by the descent into experience, and the only acceptable definition of virtue is something uncontaminated by the forms of linguistic expression. *Epistle I.vi.* had shown the effects of rigid and corrupt social forms on Pope's attitude toward language: a distrust of high rhetoric, a wariness of the capacity of language to harden into meaningless gesture. But the conception of virtue that Pope holds for much of *Epistle I.i.* fosters a more radical distrust. In the second half of the poem, Pope forgoes all attempts to define or image virtue, with one telling exception:

> Yet every child another song will sing,
> "Virtue, brave boys! 'tis Virtue makes a King."
> *True, conscious Honour is to feel no sin,*
> *He's arm'd without that's innocent within.*
>
> (91-94, my emphasis)

The naturalness and spontaneity of this may be attractive, but its childish simplicity, its rigid and assertive innocence, and its brittleness of expression imply a notion of virtue as a state of utter purity and complete inwardness. Virtue is virtue, in this view, and if a man is spotless enough to possess it he knows so.

This belief in the purely intuitive nature of "conscious honor" makes language in itself problematic, and almost from the opening of the poem this latent perception shapes the style of Pope's discourse. Pope is continually requiring language to do more than it can, striving for an extreme plainness of diction that only points up more clearly the nature of the problem, the irreducible presence of even the most transparent and Sprat-like idiom:

> What right, what true, what fit, we justly call,
> Let this be all my care — for this is All.

Periphrasis is inevitable. Not the thing itself, but words about the thing are what Pope is condemned to. Thus the acquisition of virtue seen under the aspect of time becomes "Life's instant business." Or attributes and effects are substituted for a definition of the task of virtue:

> That task, which as we follow, or despise,
> The eldest is a fool, the youngest wise;
> Which done, the poorest can no wants endure,
> And which not done, the richest must be poor.
>
> (43-46)

Or truisms are advanced as maxims:

> Not to go back, is somewhat to advance,
> And men must walk at least before they dance.
>
> (53-54)

The notion that virtue is purity, and that knowledge of virtue is necessarily intuitive and private, has further implications. First, as Pope's wariness of even congenial sects shows (23-24), there is the threat of a multiplicity of inner lights; like *Epistle I.vi.*, the poem abounds with counselors, most of whom are false. The bold assurance in London's voice, for example, and its replacement of a genuinely pious "saving doctrine," demonstrate the kind of power available to enterprising meanness and hollow but steadfastly held values: "Get Mony, Mony still!/ And then let Virtue follow, if she will." The privacy of the inner light can also foster complacency and an unwillingness to recognize one's connections with the real world of impure values and mixed experience. Here, as elsewhere, Pope's images of retirement are revealing:

> ST JOHN, whose love indulg'd my labours past
> Matures my present, and shall bound my last!
> Why will you break the Sabbath of my days?
> Now sick alike of Envy and of Praise.
> Publick too long, ah let me hide my Age!
> See modest Cibber now has left the Stage:
> Our Gen'rals now, retir'd to their Estates,
> Hang their old Trophies o'er the Garden gates,
> In Life's cool evening satiate of applause,
> Nor fond of bleeding, ev'n in BRUNSWICK's cause.
>
> (1-10)

The dubious precedent of Cibber, the self-satisfied smugness caught in the now-decorative trophies, and the easy Latinate "prettiness" of the penultimate line create an image of retirement that shows it to be a form of escape, not merely from the corruption and moral complexity of London or the world, but from the uncertainty and ceaseless process of life itself. Whether or not "the Sabbath of my days" refers to Pope's age (as Warburton argued), it surely refers to a complacent and permanent withdrawal from the business of living that a man can never enjoy within this life. It is the product of avoidance and fantasy — a sabbath of the poet's daze — and not of clear perceptions and substantial self-knowledge. If Pope devotes the body of his poem to a schematic and powerfully satiric vision of the world, he offers in its opening lines a contrasting vision of placidly escapist retirement.

Contrast, of course, need not imply contradiction and in this case it most certainly does not. Pope's vision of retirement and his vision of the world are both the product of schematic rather than substantial knowledge, knowledge that implies a radical isolation from the world and a radical simplification of both that world and the knower. The apparent contrast between retirement and satire masks a deeper resemblance, and the implications of this are crucial. First, Pope recapitulates *in propria persona* the very pattern of apparent contrast and underlying sameness that he had discovered in the world. Second, this recapitulation constitutes an unmasking of one last resemblance posing as contrast, the resemblance between the poet — a figure of retired leisure or visionary scorn — and the world from which he claims to withdraw. Pope thus seems inevitably implicated in the world he satirizes, the world from which he strives assiduously to separate himself.

The closing address to Lord Bolingbroke treats these problems, and most of the other problems raised by the poem, in the context of the relationship between Pope and his "Guide, Philosopher, and Friend." The main subject of this address was also Plato's subject in the *Meno:* the communication of that most inward of qualities, virtue. "It amounts to the question," says Socrates, "whether the good men of this and former times have known how to hand on to someone else the goodness that was in themselves, or whether on the contrary it is not something that can be handed over, or that one man can receive from another."[24] Lord Bolingbroke has disturbed the sabbath of Pope's days, and it is to him that the poet, now painfully aware of his own inconsistency, looks for instruction.

Bolingbroke, though amusedly aware of the irregularities in Pope's dress, seems curiously blind to the disorders of his mind, and above all to that contradictoriness with which Pope intensifies Horace's portrait of indecorousness:

You never change one muscle of your face,

> You think this Madness but a common case,
> Nor one to Chanc'ry, nor to Hales apply;
> Yet hang your lip, to see a Seam awry!
> Careless how ill I with myself agree;
> Kind to my dress, my figure, not to Me.
> Is this my Guide, Philosopher, and Friend?
> This, He who loves me, and who ought to mend?
> Who ought to make me (what he can, or none,)
> That man divine whom Wisdom calls her own....
>
> (171-80)

Pope's tone is these lines modulates from a cool observation of Bolingbroke's apparent indifference to a self-indulgent and petulantly intimate rebuke. Pope had italicized in his Horatian text the phrases "[de] *te pendentis, te suspicientis.*" The detail with which Pope observes Bolingbroke's slightest reaction to him, and the irritation captured in the repetition of "ought" (178-79), reveal not a respectful deference but an extreme and dependent passivity, an almost literal "hanging on" Bolingbroke's guidance, which Horace does not begin to suggest. A passage from a letter to Lord Bathurst, written in a moment of dejection, helps to clarify Pope's attitude:

> But dull as I am, I wake a little at the thought of you, I dream of you still, and you are the object of my Dotings; like an old Woman that loves the man that had her maiden-head: You animated my Youth, my Lord, Comfort my age!...'tis the serious Wish of my heart, to be loved as much as you can, and protected by you. I feel the want of you in all my little distresses; if any other hurts me, I am like a Child that comes to complain to its best friend who has humourd it always; and if I play the fool, I want to complain to you against my self: I know you to be so much a better friend to me than myself.... Your Lordship is almost my only Prop.[25]

The images with which Pope describes himself, and the fervency of his language, create a picture of dependence and passivity that perfectly annotates the appeal to Bolingbroke.

Such a state is not adequate to the task Pope wishes to

accomplish: the attainment of philosophic self-possession, consistency of self. Rather, as the confusion of person in the letter shows (" 'tis the serious Wish of my heart, to be lovd as much as you can"), it is a state in which the self eagerly surrenders to identification, and this is precisely what occurs in the last lines of the poem. As Pope looks more anxiously to Bolingbroke, he also looks away from himself. His image of an ideal future self merges with a vision of Bolingbroke into a full-blown fantasy of perfection that sublimely leaves behind the frustrations of human limits. Such a man as Pope envisions would be

> Great without Title, without Fortune bless'd,
> Rich ev'n when plunder'd, honour'd while oppress'd,
> Lov'd without youth, and follow'd without power,
> At home tho' exil'd, free, tho' in the Tower.
>
> (181-84)

That Bolingbroke was not actually in the Tower provides external corroboration of the tone and meaning of the passage. As the series of violently antithetical abstractions helps to show, the portrait is not of an actual but of an idealized — a purely rhetorical — being.[26] The next lines, following the full stop after "Tower," show Pope toppling the edifice he has created and descending back among the sons of earth:

> In short, that reas'ning, high, immortal Thing,
> Just less than Jove, and much above a King,
> Nay half in Heav'n — except (what's mighty odd)
> A Fit of Vapours clouds this Demi-God.
>
> (185-88)

The lines ironically acknowledge the evasion of reality they climax. They are an acceptance of limits and responsibility, a recognition that — in the creation of the self — to ask that one's "little bark attendant sail" is to do oneself less than justice. Pope has rejected the possibility of merely willing virtue. He must also move beyond the passivity that only identifies with another, and come ultimately to substantial self-knowledge and to the awareness that, even if he does not know how, he must make his own soul. Jove can supply life and means, Horace says elsewhere, but the equal soul I will provide for myself.[27]

The vision of the Good or the acquisition of the equal soul requires an effort of the self. Meno is not Socrates, nor Pope Lord Bolingbroke. All a Socrates or a St. John can do, and it is a great deal, is to draw one out of habitual rigidity by being an insistent presence and a pattern who, "while he bids thee, sets th'Example too" (109). Socrates, in the oblique style that his theory of knowledge and conception of the Good require, says as much at the end of the *Meno*:

> If all we have said in this discussion, and the questions we have asked, have been right, virtue will be acquired neither by nature nor by teaching. Whoever has it gets it by divine dispensation without taking thought, *unless he be the kind of statesman who can create another like himself.... Where Virtue is concerned, such a man would be...a solid reality among shadows.*[28]

Like the Socratic dialogue, Pope's poem is a prelude to virtue. Each becomes fully "achieved" only in the quality of the life, the fineness of the consciousness, that it serves initially to liberate. The reshaping of liberated energies and awareness into a moral identity must be done by oneself.

But in what context can this moral identity be created? Pope, writing of the happiness that virtue affords, gives one answer in *An Essay on Man*: " 'Tis no where to be found, or ev'ry where" (IV.16). This suggests that the world Pope has condemned as hopelessly enslaved and inconsistent, that seems to offer no role for the virtuous man, nevertheless constitutes his likeliest scene of happiness. *Epistle I.i.* is, in these terms, a recapturing under harsher circumstances — and on a more inward level — of the vision of charity that the *Essay on Man* develops in its last Epistle. "Publick too long, ah let me hide my Age!" Pope wrote at the beginning of *Epistle I.i*; the fantasy-union with Bolingbroke at the close is the last version of that escapist retirement from which Bolingbroke originally roused him (in a witty recompense of the opening of *An Essay on Man*). Not to acknowledge one's part in the world, to attempt rather to hide it, is to reenact its principal failing: entrapment in partial vision, or in a series of partial and unrelated visions (inconsistency). When Pope acknowledges his own genuine inconsistency, the argument runs, he prepares for the final recognition that self-awareness can come only from other-awareness, the private good only from the public.

But there is no such final recognition in *Epistle I.i*, only the discarding of one more illusion. The poem reveals in its clearest form the pattern of irreconcilable contradiction that informs much of Pope's major poetry. In a corrupt society, the public good can be pursued only through satire or retirement, both of which are conceived as positive social and political acts (satire tries to inculcate in the world at large those values that the community of retirement preserves from extinction). But *Epistle I.i.*, and the *Imitations* as a whole, show Pope to be caught between surrender of himself to a corrupt world and radical isolation from it. At first, these extremes do not seem irreconcilable, for retirement lies between them. But *Epistle I.i* dramatizes Pope's discovery that no such middle ground exists. Pope himself displays the inconsistency that besets the Londoners, and not least in this alternation between detachment and engagement; and his retirement is also shown to be a form of their mad individualism and self-entrapment. Isolation from society and surrender to it are not the extremes of a spectrum of possibility near the middle of which lies a rational compromise. Rather, they are mutually contradictory states, either of which taken alone becomes equivalent to the other, resulting in a total loss of distinction. There is no "between" and no possible choice between these extremes.

This pattern is not simply political or social, determining only the poet's relation to society; it governs the world of his later poetry in almost every sphere. Pope answers the dilemma it poses with an effort of complex apprehension that strives to acknowledge inevitable contradictions while neither choosing between their terms nor searching vainly for a nonexistent way to reconcile them. By the end of *Epistle I.i,* Pope has not found an acceptable public role but discovered that none exists *and* that his isolation is potentially disastrous. Nor does Pope acknowledge, as he had in *Epistle II.ii,* an individual genius or "God of Nature" who provides a ground of being for the contradictions of human nature. Rather, he replaces the mere alternation between apparent extremes with a full and simultaneous recognition of genuine contradictions in his own human nature:

> (each Opinion with the next at strife,
> One ebb and flow of follies all my Life)
> I plant, root up, I build, and then confound,
> Turn round to square, and square again to round.
> (167-70)

Pope's movement from simplistic isolation to self-division and self-knowledge is matched by the development of his friendship with Lord Bolingbroke. At first, Bolingbroke is imaged not merely as a patron or friend but as a kind of benevolent and accommodating aether in which the poet lives and moves and has his being: "ST JOHN, whose love indulg'd my labours past/Matures my present, and shall bound my last" (1-2). As in *Epistle II.ii,* however, a salutary disruption, a process of separation, thrusts Pope into a relationship that is more mature than the passivity of these opening lines or the fantasy-identification of the conclusion. And just as Pope's challenging questions to the Colonel at the end of *Epistle II.ii.* were designed to spur him to self-questioning and self-knowledge, so, in *Epistle I.i,* Pope must learn this lesson himself. When, at last, he does so, he does not reconcile himself to the world, or discover significant and shapely unity in his own spiritual life. But he does demystify himself; he does enjoy, for the moment, substantial — if humbling — self-knowledge. At precisely this moment, the poem concludes.

The remarkable range of Pope's self-identification in this poem, his acknowledged connections with both the madmen who throng the world and the idea of humanity manifest in Lord Bolingbroke, constitutes a kind of solution to the problem of the satirist's Olympian stance. The world of *Epistle I.i.* is fully as schematic and dehumanized as anything we have thus far seen, but while Pope stands apart and describes it, he also describes his own place in it. The effect is to generalize the figure of the poet while disclosing as well the connections of the prevalent social madness with the contradictions of human nature. Pope allows us to see both the ludicrous and the heroic aspects of his effort to create an authentic self, and to see, even more intensely than in the other epistles, that this effort is never complete. Indeed, these two elements — the replacement of a reconciling middle way with the recognition of irreconcilable doubleness; the emphasis on temporal process and thus on time as a potentially redemptive medium — account for much of the special difficulty and the special achievement of Pope's later poetry.

Finally, we can see in this poem an important link between the Horatian epistles and the *Epistles to Several Persons* (and, more obliquely, *An Essay on Man*). The discovery in which the *Epistles to Several Persons* culminate, that the centrally human may be glimpsed through the particular and individual, allows Pope, in the *Imitations*, to stage an exemplary drama of the individual's quest for the human

within himself, a drama that in poem after poem recalls
Montaigne's famous remark: "Chaque homme porte la
forme entière de l'humaine condition."[29] Yet Pope only
rarely discovers, and then only in a limited way, that "thus
far was right" (*Arbuthnot*, 419). For Pope's principal identity
in the epistles, and the principal source of his symbolic
power, rests with his continuing quest for self-knowledge
and with the relationship of that questing self to the mixed
humanity it discovers.

4 History and Vision: The Satiric Pattern

i. Introduction: History and Vision

WHEN Spenser's Redcross Knight is at last granted a vision of the New Jerusalem, he is simultaneously burdened with a full perception of the world's vanity. Momentarily despairing, he implores his aged guide:

> O let me not (quoth he) then turn againe
> Back to the world, whose ioyes so fruitlesse are;
> But let me here for aye in peace remaine,
> Or streight way on that last long voyage fare,
> That nothing may my present hope empare.

The Knight's guide, Heavenly Contemplation, responds, "That may not be," whereupon the knight resumes, as he must, his worldly role and duties.[1] Pope, of course, is not Spenser; his emphasis falls on the vision of vanity, and his scene is less insistently "the world." But this conversion from apocalyptic vision to qualified worldly involvement — or more simply, from seeing through the world to going on living — is nevertheless a movement that is central to both the *Epistles to Several Persons* and the Horatian epistles. Whether playful, as in the epistle *To Burlington*, or more darkly serious, as in some of the imitations, the reductive and schematic vision is continually qualified, integrated into a self that proves large and flexible enough to contain it without being identified with it: a self that is, in part, won back to the world it had begun by knowing and rejecting, even if it is won back only by acknowledging its kinship with that world and thus its own flawed humanity. In these cases, Pope's reconciling myth lies in precisely this acknowledgment, and the reconciliation is, as it must be for a man of such vision as the poet can claim, imperfect. For these acts of humanization do not negate the apocalyptic impulse but exist in uneasy tension with it. The Redcross Knight does not forget what he has seen from "the highest Mount."

Pope's satires are the structural antithesis of his epistles. They do not humanize the apocalyptic stance but instead dramatize its inevitable emergence from a relationship that has been eroded in the course of the poem. This relationship is, as we might expect, initially two-sided and precarious. In *Satire II.i.* and the *Epilogue to the Satires,* Pope begins by engaging in dialogue with a representative of the very world he is also satirically attacking. The satiric stance (however mild the attack) exists simultaneously with a communal or participatory stance (however cool the dialogue). For a brief moment, the poet is both the moral critic of the world and one of its genuine citizens. In *Satire II.ii.*, Pope begins by praising the austerity of life that is the theme of Bethel's sermon while at the same time entering a personal disclaimer: "(A doctrine sage, but truly none of mine)" (3).

This initial double attitude, which strives to accommodate both the moderate use of worldly things (as in Pope's image of his retired estate) and the stoic detachment of a Bethel, nevertheless ends as something very close to an unqualified transcendence of all worldly concerns. Similarly, *Satire II.i.* and the *Epilogue to the Satires* dramatize a breakdown of dialogue and a progressive simplification of both the poet's identity and his relation to the world. In the *Epilogue*, the dialogue breaks off as Pope, superbly asserting values that are the very antithesis of the Friend's, approaches the role of a moral hero who is homeless in a corrupt world. In the earlier *Satire II.i,* the dialogue is sustained but its communicative function is, at the end, wholly lost. Pope and the

Friend are stil speaking, but they are speaking entirely different languages. Whatever its particular form, the pattern in each satire is one of inevitable breakdown of relationship, involving a simplification of the poet's identity and of his way of seeing the world. Stoic denial and moderate use, moral judgment and communal participation, satire and dialogue seem at first to be compatible. But each poem moves toward an inescapable choice that undermines the possibility of such a double attitude and forces the poet into an unremittingly visionary solitude, an unremittingly apocalyptic stance.

Few of Pope's writings can be called apocalyptic in the full sense of that word, although, as Maynard Mack has said, his poetry "has apocalyptic mutterings in it from his earliest years."[2] But insofar as *apocalyptic* refers purely to the way in which a poet sees, it is applicable to all those moments of detachment and schematic knowledge — satiric and nonsatiric — that appear in Pope's poems of the 1730s. For Pope's poetry frequently implicates into its prevailing satiric and epistolary texture aspects of what we may consider, rightly or wrongly, to be the grander forms of poetic utterance: tragedy, epic, apocalyptic vision. In the closing lines of *To Burlington*, for example, the verse acquires an unmistakably epic tone, the tone of a poet who sees the particulars of history in all their intrinsic worth and usefulness, but also sees them contributing to a larger purpose, an historical pattern or destiny that lends them a significance beyond the intrinsic. If we can see an epic stance making its way into the limited quarters of the address to Burlington, then we can also see that what governs the earlier passage on Virro, Sir Visto, and Bubo (13-22) is a limited form of apocalyptic vision, a perspective from which historical particulars are not in creative tension with an overall plan but wholly subordinated to it. Apocalypse, in this sense, is the scheme with which the imagination is left when historical particulars lose their substantiality, their intrinsic density and meaningfulness, and become merely a "vast involuntary throng."[3]

But *apocalyptic* does not describe simply a way of seeing; it also implies certain attributes of what is seen — notably, its scope. The pattern disclosed in apocalyptic vision is a pattern that underlies the world, the whole of human history, rather than a merely local scene. Thus the fourth book of *The Dunciad* can be properly called apocalyptic, but this cannot be said — despite the similarity in mode of vision — of the description of Virro and the others in *To Burlington*. This same distinction can be drawn, in a more general way, between the satires and the epistles. Where we speak of schematic knowledge or vision in the epistles, we may apply the term *apocalyptic* to the more overt confrontation of the entire human scene in the satires. For the same reason, we may substitute "historical" for "substantial" in speaking of the form that substantial knowledge takes in the satires. Thus the epistles move from schematic to substantial knowledge, while the satires — both reversing this movement and widening the scope of its terms — move from historical knowledge to apocalyptic vision.

The main features of Pope's apocalyptic satire are familiar. There is, above all, the tendency to see "principles" rather than mere instances of vice and folly, and to perceive a world driven by what a scholastic might call "modes" of Dulness. Since the substance of experience is thus reduced to abstractions, and since abstractions readily absorb concrete facts, the world is often perceived as a corrupt totality. In the *Epilogue to the Satires*, Pope describes Vice in these terms:

> Her Birth, her Beauty, Crowds and Courts confess,
> Chaste Matrons praise her, and grave Bishops bless:
> In golden Chains the willing World she draws,
> And hers the Gospel is, and hers the Laws:
> Mounts the Tribunal, lifts her scarlet head,
> And sees pale Virtue carted in her stead!

(I.145-50)

The sense of crisis that is normally associated with the apocalyptic may, as in this passage, be explicitly present, or it may be present merely by implication. That is, to see through the substance of worldly experience is also to see through the fullness of time, whether or not the consequent imminence of the end is made explicit. If the world is reduced to mere pattern, "the end," perceptually speaking, is now, and it is with the poet's perception, his knowledge, that we are concerned. Confronting this world, the poet confronts as well his own alienation. He is "sick alike of Envy and of Praise" (*Epistle I.i.*4), and he approaches a quasi-divine transcendence of the chaos of the world and the chaos of his own character. The poet also subordinates all to absolute concerns, for the last day, as best he can tell, is today: " 'Nothing is Sacred now but Villany' " (*Epilogue to the Satires*, II. 170). A man of lucid — indeed, at times too lucid — perception, he is also a figure of absolute principles, grim courage, and world-weariness.

Just as he had to earn the substantial knowledge with which the epistles conclude, so, in the satires, Pope does not immediately articulate the apocalyptic vision but is gradually driven to it in the course of the poem. Indeed, as we should expect, Pope dramatizes his resistance to that vision almost as strongly as he asserts its inevitability. That resistance most often takes the form of a strong attachment to concrete, historical reality. As an example, a prose advertisement of considerable historical specificity was affixed to *Satire II.i.* at one point in its publication, and the original title of the *Epilogue to the Satires* (shortened and incorporated in later versions) itself named the poem's occasion: nothing less than an *annus mirabilis* of vice, *One Thousand Seven Hundred and Thirty Eight.* More significantly, Pope begins *Satire II.i.* and the *Epilogue* by intensely engaging the historical particulars from which he is forced gradually to separate himself. In *Satire II.i.* Pope departs from Horace by not merely listing complaints against his satire (as Horace also had) but by

introducing specific individuals as well: Peter, Chartres,
Lord Fanny. The issue of general *versus* particular satire has
usually been discussed, sometimes by Pope's interlocutors
and adversaries, in terms of the poet's willingness to wound.
But particular satire, though it may have angered more of
Pope's contemporaries than a visionary tableau like the
Triumph of Vice in the first dialogue of the *Epilogue*,
nevertheless expresses impulses contrary to — or resisting
— that scornful disdain of the world with which the satirist
of particulars is usually also charged.

For Pope, to put it simply, needed the world as much as he
needed to be free of it. Consider the lines from *Satire II.i.* in
which he describes his virtuous aloofness:

> Yes, while I live, no rich or noble knave
> Shall walk the World, in credit, to his grave.
> To Virtue only and her Friends, a Friend,
> The World beside may murmur, or commend.
> *Know, all the distant Din that World can keep*
> *Rolls o'er my Grotto, and but sooths my Sleep.*
> (119-24, my emphasis)

The final couplet is not a statement of impregnability or
unconcern, or at least it is not only that. Pope might have
said, after all, that the world's din does not *disturb* his sleep.
But the poet's sleep, unlike the "rest" urged by the Friend in
this poem (or by Despair in Book I of *The Faerie Queene*), is
neither an annihilation of personal identity nor a repression
of the claims of the world. It is a repose generated,
paradoxically, by the tension between the self and the world,
earned by the persistent effort to keep either from collapsing
into the other. Unless we are to understand the speaker of
the opening lines as a *faux naif* rather than a *naif*, we must
see certain of Pope's alterations of Horace contributing to
his implicit belief in this double identity, in the possibility
of being both satirist and citizen, as in the addition of the
parenthetical "I scarce can think it, but am told", and the

incredulous repetition of "There are." The effect of these phrases is to subordinate the differences between objections to an expression of surprise at their very presence. The sleep enjoyed by Pope at Twickenham, in his "little House, with Trees a-row,/ And like its Master, very low," is the sounder for his abiding consciousness of that world which was, however inadequate in itself, an inescapable condition of his fullest poetic identity.

Another way in which Pope resists the apocalyptic vision, and visionary singleness of identity, is to emphasize the conflicting forces within his own character. Pope accomplishes this, in part, by making certain changes in his Horatian original: saying of himself what Horace says of Lucilius, or expanding Horace's autobiographical interludes to complicate further an already complex self-portrait.[4] At one point in *Satire II.i.*, for example, Pope replaces Lucilius with two figures, "downright *Shippen*" and "old *Montagne*," as precedents for self-revelation, adding that such self-revelation is also something of a social act: "In them, as certain to be lov'd as seen,/ The Soul stood forth, nor kept a Thought within" (53-54). And he concludes the passage with a self-portrait that expresses more directly than its source in Horace the ambiguous identity of the poet:

> My Head and Heart thus flowing thro' my Quill,
> Verse-man or Prose-man, term me which you will,
> Papist or Protestant, or both between,
> Like good *Erasmus* in an honest Mean,
> In Moderation placing all my Glory,
> While Tories call me Whig, and Whigs a Tory.
>
> (63-68)

A passage such as this, in which the succession of roles suggests sheer possibility of identity and the use of participles sheer process — and which picks up in structure and in the image of "flowing" the earlier "I love to pour out all myself" — contrasts strikingly with the satiric statements that follow it and with the heroic declarations, also intensified from Horace, that stress Pope's inflexibility of vision (e.g., 105-20).

The "Moderation" claimed by Pope as his glory and natural state of mind is, in the satires as in the epistles, no mere compromise but a complex relationship of extremes. To describe the full range of Pope's stances toward the world in the 1730s would be to describe nearly every point on a spectrum stretching between the superb isolation of the apocalyptic satirist and the more than communal bond with mankind that is glimpsed near the close of *An Essay on Man*. That accomplished, however, we should have to acknowledge that the image of a spectrum — particularly its built-in suggestion that a moderate stance lies somewhere near the middle — had outlived its usefulness. The claims of the self and the claims of the world are contradictory terms that cannot be resolved in a simple way. Pope's satire is not a resistance to community as such, but to an idea of the communal that excludes real individuality. And those acts of humanization that characterize the epistles do not qualify individuality as such, but an idea of individuality that claims to be able to do without the world and that threatens to lose its own genuineness by perceiving the world as uniformly insubstantial. Genuine individuality and genuine community depend on a relatedness that harbors a paradox at its center. Pope tries to save that relatedness and to recover that paradox. Such a paradoxical nature is radically impure, but this is an enabling impurity; opposing claims, insofar as either is taken alone, will "snatch the Man away." This is precisely what happens in the satires. "The Man," the poet, becomes simplified to an emblematic moral hero, by the close of these poems, without a community to speak to or a world in which to live. If the epistles dramatize the recovery of human complexity, the satires dramatize the inevitable emergence of visionary simplicity. And they dramatize as well both the moral authority of the visionary satirist and the human cost of assuming that authority.

ii. The Satiric Pattern: Satire II.i.

Maynard Mack has remarked that the structure of *Satire II.i.,* Pope's earliest imitation of Horace (1733), "is in a very real sense a function of the modulations in tone that it takes to get from the opening verses" through the roles of hero and *vir bonus* and back to the "voice of the *ingenu,* surprised and pained that he should be thought to have any but the noblest aims."[5] These tonal modulations, in the satires, reflect a disclosure rather than a development of the poet's character. As the poet responds to the objections of the shallow and timid Friend, he gradually reveals the depth of that inner life that is casually alluded to in the earlier exchanges. This structure of challenge and response is clear in the sustained dialogues, *Satire II.i.* and the two dialogues of the *Epilogue to the Satires,* and it appears obliquely, though no less significantly, in *Satire II.ii.* and *An Epistle to Dr. Arbuthnot.*

What, precisely, is disclosed in the course of *Satire II.i.?* First, Pope's reasons for writing. From the half-humorous excuse of insomnia, through a milder statement of Juvenal's *difficile est saturam non scribere* (14), Pope moves to several extended explanations. In the first of these, he admits to a passion for self-revelation:

> Each Mortal has his Pleasure,
>
> .   .   .   .
>
> I love to pour out all myself, as plain
> As downright *Shippen,* or as old *Montagne.*
>
> $\qquad\qquad\qquad\qquad$ (45, 51-52)

But this dilates almost imperceptibly into a more impersonal and public ambition, to be the moral historian of his time:

> In this impartial Glass, my Muse intends
> Fair to expose myself, my Foes, my Friends;

> Publish the present Age, but where my Text
> Is Vice too high, reserve it for the next.
>
>   (57-60)

At the same time, Pope establishes a context for his satire, which is no longer wholly identified with the kind of poetry he writes but claimed merely as his weapon. And although satire is at first a personal weapon — "But touch me, and no Minister so sore" (76) — it soon becomes part of the whole armor of virtue that he superbly assumes:

> What? arm'd for *Virtue* when I point the Pen,
> Brand the bold Front of shameless, guilty Men,
> Dash the proud Gamester in his gilded Car,
> Bare the mean Heart that lurks beneath a Star;
> Can there be wanting to defend Her Cause,
> Lights of the Church, or Guardians of the Laws?
>
>   (105-110)

As the accounts of various motives succeed one another, so do the poet's definitions, both explicit and implicit, of poetry. It is satire, self-revelation, impartial history ("my Muse intends"), and finally, moral revelation, "grave *Epistles,* bringing Vice to light" (151). Thus, as Pope's reasons for writing expand to involve the whole moral man rather than simply the compulsive rhymester, and as poetry (in his definitions) approaches the purity of moral assertion, the two — man and poetry — begin to converge. The central issue of the poem thus changes from conduct to identity, from what Pope ought to do to who he is. Self and poetry, being and saying, stand or fall together. The poet's implicit assumption of this unity helps to account for the naive tone of the opening lines. But as the Friend persists in his effort to separate him from poetry, Pope is forced to articulate the moral perception that unites them.

If the structure of the poem is a function of its modulations in tone, the energy for those modulations is generated by the series of confrontations between Pope and his "Council

learned in the Law" (8).[6] Pope addresses the Friend as "both
sage and free," but the Friend seems rather stingy with his
advice: "I'd write no more" (11). He is not so much reluctant
to give free advice, however, as he is wary of committing
himself on a legal question that is also a political issue. Thus
he quickly shifts ground from law to medicine, offering his
own prescription with an offhand vagueness designed to
attest at once to his benevolence and his incompetence: "But
talk with *Celsus, Celsus* will advise/Hartshorn, or something
that shall close your eyes" (19-20). The rest of the poem
shows that the moral implications of the final phrase should
not be overlooked. When the Friend does take it upon
himself to advise, he never strays from the securely
conventional: "Lettuce and Cowslip Wine; *Probatum Est.*" If
Pope must write, "write Caesar's Praise:/ You'll gain at least
a *Knighthood*, or the *Bays*" (21-22). The Friend's use of
"Caesar" (since Pope himself mentions George in the next
lines) should probably be read as an attempt to preserve
legal impersonality by avoiding even such partisanship as
naming the current Caesar might imply. Yet "George"
would also be less appropriate to the Friend's character, for
it is the generic "Caesar" — whoever is in power — that he
serves and advises Pope to praise.

The form of the Friend's counsel is as damaging as its
content. As the lines on Celsus suggest, nearly every offer of
advice is in fact a referral. Unlike Horace's Trebatius, who
merely quotes from law, the Friend cites precedents as well:
"It stands on record, that in *Richard's* Times/ A Man was
hang'd for very honest Rhymes" (145-46). And just as here he
slips into legal jargon, "*Edwardi. Sext.* or *Prim. & quint. Eliz.*,"
so in advising Pope to flatter the royal family the Friend
slips into the language of sycophantic song:

> Then all your Muse's softer Art display,
> Let *Carolina* smooth the tuneful Lay,
> Lull with *Amelia's* liquid Name the Nine,

And sweetly flow through all the Royal Line.
                                    (29-32)

The Friend, in short, lacks a self substantial enough to be
capable of advice, of becoming engaged at any level deeper
than the blandly conventional. He refers to other authorities,
collapses into his subjects, acts out his own advice, and
becomes the alternatives he suggests. The Friend displays
throughout an inability to consider experience freshly, or to
animate a role with the energies of a genuine self. As a
result, he is little more than a sequence of roles whose
unifying principle is precisely their continuing evidence of
an abdication of true identity. This dissolving of self in
quiescence and passivity, moreover, is the burden of the
Friend's advice to Pope. Both Horace and Pope introduce
the theme of sleep early in their poems, but the Friend,
unlike Horace's Trebatius, really has no other alternative to
the writing of satire. "But you might write of himself
[Caesar], at once just and valiant, as wise Lucilius did of
Scipio," urges Trebatius. Pope's Friend offers a soporific for
the Muses rather than an alternative labor: "Lull with
Amelia's liquid Name the Nine."[7]

The relationship between self and role in *Satire II.i.* is
analogous to that between the spirit and the letter of the law.
From the early and pointedly ambiguous announcement,
"I come to Council learned in the Law," to the hissing of the
plaintiff that closes the poem, Pope vivifies the Friend's
legal terms with the eloquence of moral vision. Pope plays
repeatedly on the word *cause*, reminding us that a legal
proceeding without a spiritual center is a hollow form:

> Can there be wanting to defend Her Cause,
> Lights of the Church, or Guardians of the Laws?
>
>   .   .   .   .
>
> And I not strip the Gilding off a Knave,
> Up-plac'd, un-pension'd, no Man's Heir, or Slave?

> I will, or perish in the gen'rous Cause.
> Hear this, and tremble! you who 'scape the Laws.
>
> (109-10, 115-18)

And the Friend's timid warning, "Laws are explain'd by Men
— so have a care" (144), is countered by the poet's commitment
to a principle of Virtue whose force swells his scornful
challenge: "This is my Plea, on this I rest my *Cause* —/ What
saith my Council learned in the *Laws*?" (141-42, my emphasis).
With this last, Pope has appropriated the Friend's legal role
as well as his moral authority.[8] For the poet does not simply
or scornfully reject the law as inadequate to his high
concerns, but insists that the meaningfulness of the law
depends on the fusion of its forms with the spirit of those
concerns. In thus becoming a legal as well as a moral
spokesman, Pope leaves the Friend with nothing. The
Friend moves from authority to irrelevance, while the
authority of the world to which Pope initially appealed ends
by being discovered within himself.

Yet this is the authority of a world different from the
Friend's. Pope's relationship to the "real" world of corruption,
intrigue, and folly has been gradually eroded in the course
of the poem. Consider the closing lines:

> *P. Libels* and *Satires*! lawless Things indeed!
> But grave *Epistles*, bringing Vice to light,
> Such as a *King* might read, a *Bishop* write,
> Such as Sir *Robert* would approve —
>
> *F.* Indeed?
> The Case is alter'd — you may then proceed.
> In such a Cause the Plaintiff will be hiss'd,
> My Lords the Judges laugh, and you're dismiss'd.
>
> (150-56)

Pope pursues the moral issue more directly than Horace.
His final claim, as one critic has observed, is based "upon a
conception of an ideally ordered world where kings and
ministers do read satire and do not think it any reflection on

themselves."⁹ Nor does the Friend's apparent agreement
demonstrate his conversion to Pope's values; it merely
reveals his conditioned response to Pope's hierarchy of
official approval and his knowledge that the justice dispensed
by the courts is ultimately a political commodity.¹⁰ There
will not be, it seems, any accord between the satirist and
society, nor any but a terminological conversion of society
by satire. The poem has revealed the gulf that divides them,
leaving Pope and the Friend in agreement about terms but
at opposite moral poles.

   Satire II.i. thus offers an interesting form of what Alvin
Kernan describes as the typical conclusion of satire: "Pure
satire is far rarer than the mixed kinds in which after a time
the satiric stasis is broken and the characters, both satirists
and fools, are swept forward into the miraculous transforma-
tions of comedy or the cruel dialectic of tragedy."¹¹ Pope
achieves considerable complexity of tone by implicating
both comic and tragic elements into the concluding satiric
stasis. From the Friend's perspective, a comic transformation
of opposition into agreement has indeed been achieved;
from our perspective, a parody of such an ending (This
"impure" comic ending is evident in Horace but exacerbated
in Pope). But the Friend's perspective harbors potentially
tragic consequences for Pope. In contrast to those who
"smart in *Timon* and in *Balaam*," or those who might "club
their Testers" to take the poet's life, the Friend fails utterly
to understand what Pope means. In Blake's terms, the
Friend is a negation rather than a contrary. Although the
poem deals explicitly with the threat of opposition —
notably, legal and physical opposition — its structure, and
the character of the Friend, implicitly raise the threat of a
negation of satire, a failure of mind that would deprive Pope
of any significant connection with the world, as he is
deprived of significant dialogue with the Friend. The satiric
stasis holds *in potentia* a tragic conclusion in which Pope,
suffering the consequences of assuming more than an official

"character" in the Friend, would be "dismiss'd" from a court of law but also left without a world.

The tragic conclusion is, of course, only potential, for the radical alienation of the poet is contained within a seeming accord. When such a conclusion does occur, in the *Epilogue to the Satires*, Pope grimly yet proudly accepts it. His withdrawal from the world, in Martin Price's words, "becomes a superb aloofness, the pride of a man whose moral habits are a passport to an order of experience the others have lost all power to reach":[12]

> Yes while I live, no rich or noble knave
> Shall walk the World, in credit, to his grave.
> TO VIRTUE ONLY and HER FRIENDS, A FRIEND,
> The World beside may murmur, or commend.
>
> (119-22)

These lines are followed by the description of the world's "distant Din" and its soothing effect on Pope's sleep. When read in connection with the poem's conclusion, however, they suggest that if Pope's moral habits are a passport to another order of experience, they also constitute, as he will come to acknowledge, a sentence of exile.

iii. The Drama of Resistance: Satire II.ii.

The *Epilogue to the Satires* bears something of the same relation to *Satire II.i.* that *Epistle I.i.* bears to *Epistle II.ii.* It is a radical revision that returns to the materials of the earlier poem only to bring out their harshest features and their most difficult truths and choices. Similarly, *Satire II.ii.*, which stands chronologically between *Satire II.i.* and the *Epilogue*, functions in the development of the satires much as *Epistle I.vi.* functions in the development of the epistles. *Satire II.ii.* treats major themes in an oblique manner and in a new context, and in doing so it unearths difficulties that are fully confronted only in the last poem of the genre.

When *Satire II.ii.* first appeared in 1734, it was combined with the second edition of *Satire II.i.* in a forty-two-page folio. The juxtaposition is instructive, for the two poems form a kind of diptych, *Satire II.ii.* generalizing the patterns of the earlier poem to a considerable extent by showing how thoroughly they underlie more genial and less political contexts. If the scope of *Satire II.ii.* seems at first the more limited, focusing on Bethel's discussion of temperance and on the poet's rural retirement, those limited concerns nevertheless display a surprising ability to rehearse, so to speak, in more limited and manageable quarters, responses to such large and difficult questions as how a man is to value the things of this world.

This question receives substantial answers from two people in Pope's version of *Satire II.ii.*, Bethel and the poet himself, for Pope speaks in his own person the lines that Horace had ascribed to Bethel's prototype, Ofellus (129-80 in Pope's poem). In the opening lines, which introduce Bethel's "sermon," Pope makes another alteration in Horace's text:

> What, and how great, the Virtue and the Art
> To live on little with a chearful heart,
> (A Doctrine sage, but truly none of mine)
> Lets talk, my friends....
>
> (1-4)

Where Horace had simply said of the proposed discourse, "Nec meus hic Sermo, sed quem praecipit Ofellus" ("This is not my talk, but Ofellus's teaching"), Pope is more emphatic: "(A Doctrine sage, but truly none of mine)." The disclaimer suggests that Pope groups himself with less austere types than Bethel, that he respects — but does not care to emulate — so frugal an example. At the same time, however, Pope retains, and makes strikingly concrete, Horace's warning against the effect of the appetites on "sound philosophy":

Lets talk, my friends, but talk before we dine:
Not when a gilt Buffet's reflected pride
Turns you from sound Philosophy aside;
Not when from Plate to Plate your eyeballs roll,
And the brain dances to the mantling bowl.

(4-8)

As a result, the opening image of the poet displays him in a complex posture, politely dissociating himself from the effort to "live on little with a chearful heart" and yet expressing a view of the senses and appetites that is more rigorously stoic than Horace's. At this point, against the background of Pope's double attitude, Bethel begins his sermon, which continues for roughly two thirds of the poem.

Bethel immediately strikes the contentious note of "plain truth" that characterizes much of his speech:

Go work, hunt, exercise! (he thus began)
Then scorn a homely dinner, if you can.
Your wine lock'd up, your Butler stroll'd abroad,
Or fish deny'd, (the River yet unthaw'd)
If then plain Bread and milk will do the feat,
The pleasure lies in *you*, and not the meat.

(11-16)

Bethel sounds like those persons whom one always remembers as shouting, no matter how loudly or softly they speak, and his sermon voices the hearty outrage of instinctive good sense astonished by foolish excess. He is equally affronted by miserly scrimping:

Avidien or his Wife (no matter which,
For him you'll call a dog, and her a bitch)
Sell their presented Partridges, and Fruits,
And humbly live on rabbits and on roots:
One half-pint bottle serves them both to dine,
And is at once their vinegar and wine.

(49-54)

The portrait recalls that of Old Cotta in the epistle *To Bathurst,* whose "kitchens vy'd in coolness with his grot" (182), for the parsimony of Avidien and his wife is less a husbanding of means than a contraction of spirit, just as their marriage is more a brutelike clinging together than a bond of affection. Bethel continues:

> But on some lucky day (as when they found
> A lost Bank-bill, or heard their Son was drown'd)
> At such a feast old vinegar to spare,
> Is what two souls so gen'rous cannot bear;
> Oyl, tho' it stink, they drop by drop impart,
> But sowse the Cabbidge with a bounteous heart.
>
> (55-60)

The grotesqueness of the portrait is the result of a fine management of focus and a darkening of Horace's original. Horace's wedding or birthday feast, for example, has become a celebration of another's loss or a son's death. The meanness of Avidien and his wife has not only limited their diet but destroyed their human feelings as well.

As these passages suggest, Bethel's views are strong and relatively simple. His conception of temperance is not nearly so rich with implication as Pope's will prove to be, but is largely a static conception of the middle way: "He knows to live, who keeps the middle state,/ And neither leans on this side, nor on that" (61-62). For the most part, too, Bethel is concerned with the self-sufficiency that temperance can supply:

> Who thinks that Fortune cannot change her mind,
> Prepares a dreadful Jest for all mankind!
> And who stands safest, tell me! is it he
> That spreads and swells in puff'd Prosperity,
> Or blest with little, whose preventing care
> In Peace provides fit arms against a War?
>
> (123-28)

Pope, in contrast, displays a keen awareness of the paradox of simplicity, altering Horace's opening lines, for example — "Quae virtus et quanta, boni, sit vivere parvo" — to include not only "the Virtue" but also "the Art" required for a frugality more complex than mere renunciation.

The contrast between Pope and Bethel is brought out by their attitudes toward writing. To Bethel, the facility of the mind and the soundness of the body are so closely related that poetry comes to be seen as one of the higher bodily functions. The muses, at any rate, seem to favor the fit:

> On morning wings how active springs the Mind,
> That leaves the load of yesterday behind?
> How easy ev'ry labour it pursues?
> How coming to the Poet ev'ry Muse?
> Not but we may exceed, some Holy time,
> Or tir'd in search of Truth, or search of Rhyme.
>
> (81-86)

And Bethel's own language is a true reflection of his character. "Reflection," in fact, suggests too oblique a relation between them: Bethel "always speaks his thought,/ And always thinks the very thing he ought" (129-30). Indeed, at times it is difficult to tell whether Pope is describing Bethel or his discourse:

> Hear Bethel's Sermon, one not vers'd in schools,
> But strong in sense, and wise without the rules.
>
> (9-10)

The subject, "one," may be "Sermon" as well as "Bethel," and "vers'd" may mean "rhymed" as readily as "experienced." When Bethel speaks, he speaks himself, and there is no need to distinguish too nicely between the utterance and the man. Pope, in contrast, reminds us that he is a poet (150), and that poetry is a matter of complexity and art. "Thus said our Friend," he remarks of Bethel at one point, "and what he *said*

I *sing*" (68, my emphasis). Such remarks call attention to the art of artlessness, and to the need for Pope to complicate a vision like Bethel's before he can make it his own.

Another contrast between Pope and Bethel centers on the theme of friendship, which enters the poem directly only with Pope's speech (except for an occasional remark of Bethel's) but has been implicitly and negatively defined in earlier examples of false society and spiritless communion: the "friendship" of courtly faddishness, for example (43-44); or the mean alliance of Avidien and his wife; or the notably unfestive Clergy and City feasts:

> How pale, each Worshipful and rev'rend Guest
> Rise from a Clergy, or a City, feast!
> What life in all that ample Body, say,
> What heav'nly Particle inspires the clay?

(75-78)

A feast, as the pun on "Body" makes clear, can be no more lively than its guests. One recalls the vivacity and ease of those lines translating Horace's "O noctes coenaeque deum!" that Pope added to Swift's version of *Satire II.vi.*:

> O charming Noons! and Nights divine!
> Or when I sup, or when I dine,
> My Friends above, my Folks below,
> Chatting and laughing all-a-row,
> The Beans and Bacon set before 'em,
> The Grace-cup serv'd with all decorum:
> Each willing to be pleas'd, and please,
> And even the very Dogs at ease!

(133-40)

This image of hearty conviviality, of a supremely social assembly in which the beans and bacon are properly subordinated to "The Feast of Reason and the Flow of Soul," contrasts sharply with the mere collective gluttony satirized by Bethel.

It contrasts almost as sharply, however, with Bethel's image of the temperate man, "blest with little, whose preventing care/ In Peace provides fit arms against a War" (127-28). As Michael O'Loughlin says of Bethel's Horatian prototype, there is a "certain impoverishment in Ofellus' stoic fare, in the insistence on denial instead of affirmation, on self-sufficiency instead of communion."[13] The same, with some qualification, might be said of Bethel. Pope, in contrast, avoids the notion that the chief blessing of temperance is self-sufficiency. His portrayal of rural retirement is deepened by his respect for the openness and liberality of honest friendship. Time's theft of money or property is not merely compensated but trivialized by the friendships that have managed to endure:

> Content with little, I can piddle here
> On Broccoli and mutton, round the year;
> But ancient friends, (tho' poor, or out of play)
> That touch my Bell, I cannot turn away.
>
> .   .   .   .
>
> My lands are sold, my Father's house is gone;
> I'll hire another's, is not that my own,
> And yours my friends? thro' whose free-opening gate
> None comes too early, none departs too late;
> (For I, who hold sage Homer's rule the best,
> Welcome the coming, speed the going guest.).
>
> (137-40, 155-60)

In Pope's translation of *The Odyssey*, "sage Homer's rule" is a rule not simply of hospitality but of "True friendship."[14]

Friendship was for Pope a complex and even a symbolic form of experience. It was certainly, as Maynard Mack says, nourished by "the warmth of a volatile and expressive nature."[15] Pope often says as much in his correspondence. "Nature, temper, and habit," he writes to Gay, "from my youth made me have but one strong desire.... That desire was to fix and preserve a few lasting, dependable friendships."[16] But friendship was also a type of the highest worldly involvement, a way in which one might participate in the world's business without sacrificing integrity. Indeed, an important office of friendship is precisely to serve as a check to self-sufficiency, to ensure that it does not — as it easily may — slide into haughty independence: "If a man be philosopher enough himself not [to] be tied to the world, his friendships and charities will engage him to it; *which he neither can, nor ought to break thro'.*"[17]

Pope's insistence on friendship, in *Satire II.ii.*, is only one aspect of a larger qualification of Bethel's speech; like Bethel's emphasis on self-sufficiency, it is part of a total attitude toward experience. While we are always made aware of Bethel's strong feelings of obligation — to decency, to mankind, to one's own best interests — we find in Pope a voluntary note that embraces and thus transforms obligations through the generosity with which they are assumed. "The happy and blessed state," as Epicurus wrote, is the reward of "an attitude of mind which *imposes* the limits *ordained* by nature."[18] The antithesis catches precisely the internalizing of necessity that Pope argues for in *An Essay on Man* and fully dramatizes in the imitations. Pope's conception of the mean, of the proper use of things, is thus ultimately liberating in a way that Bethel's is not, for Bethel's stance is a defensive posture. Bethel's sermon, as we might expect, is a collection of negative examples; even the remembered health of the schoolboy seems almost overwhelmed by the startling vision of "intestine war" that precedes it (69-74). There is a certain irony in speaking of Bethel's "stance" at all, for his concern not to be surprised by fortune makes him to a considerable degree her thrall. We are not free of that which we are continually striving to anticipate. Pope, on the other hand, in his lovely description of his "five acres.... of rented land," provides the perfect emblem of his skill in creating an identity that is at once more stable and more generous than Bethel's.

Nowhere is this contrast clearer than in their attitudes toward time. Bethel is repeatedly drawn toward images of past simplicity. At one point (speaking for the stomach) he recalls the innocence of youthful health, "the Schoolboy's simple fare,/ The temp'rate sleeps, and spirits light as air!" (73-74). Elsewhere, he bitterly enumerates the few relics of a vanished and more frugal era:

> Cheap eggs, and herbs, and olives still we see,
> Thus much is left of old Simplicity!
>
> (35-36)

Or he wishes such an era were his own:

> Why had not I in those good times my birth,
> E're Coxcomb-pyes or Coxcombs were on earth?
>
> (97-98)

When Bethel is not denouncing the present, or glancing wistfully at the past, he is casting an anxious eye toward the future:

> Ill Health some just indulgence may engage,
> And more, the Sickness of long Life, Old-age:
> For fainting Age what cordial drop remains,
> If our intemp'rate Youth the Vessel drains?
>
> (87-90)

It is fitting that Bethel's final statement is cast in the form of a question:

> And who stands safest, tell me? is it he
> That spreads and swells in puff'd Prosperity,
> Or blest with little, whose preventing care
> In Peace provides fit arms against a War?
>
> (125-28)

And fitting, too, that the subject of the second couplet is lost in his own preventing care. Except as an irritant, the present scarcely exists for Bethel.

In contrast, the measured serenity of Pope's lines owes much to their freedom from both nostalgia and anxiety. One example is a passage frequently cited in admiration of Pope's descriptive powers:

> From yon old wallnut-tree a show'r shall fall;
> And grapes, long-lingring on my only Wall,
> And figs, from standard and Espalier join:
> The dev'l is in you if you cannot dine.
>
> (145-48)

As Mack notes, Pope adds to Horace's picture of simplicity "a notably seventeenth-century English sense of proprietorship and place."[19] The sense of place, moreover, is richly reinforced by a sense of time. The "old wallnut-tree," the "long-lingring" grapes and carefully cultivated fig trees express at once a continuity that includes man and a responsiveness that meets his momentary needs and desires. This image of a natural scene quietly transfigured by human art is an emblem not merely of an acceptance of natural process, a surrender to time and loss, but also of their modest human redemption. And time and loss may be compensated in other ways as well. "I am pleased," Pope wrote to Ralph Allen in 1736, "to think my Trees will afford Shade and Fruit to Others, when I shall want them no more. And it is no sort of grief to me, that those others will not be Things of my own poor Body, but it is enough they are Creatures of the same Species, and made by the same hand that made me."[20]

This image of Pope's retired scene would have provided a tranquil and edifying conclusion to the poem, but Pope introduces a jarring note in the speech of Swift (for which there is no precedent in Horace):

"Pray heav'n it last! (cries Swift) as you go on;
"I wish to God this house had been your own:
"Pity! to build, without a son or wife:
"Why, you'll enjoy it only all your life." —

(161-64)

This is anxiety become ludicrous. Bethel had urged that one prepare for inevitable bad times by expecting them and by living in a providently frugal way against their appearance. Swift is a more intense version of Bethel. He cannot endure time and change but, striving for certainty, longs for a degree of permanence that is simply unavailable in human life. "*Man?* and *for ever?*" Pope had replied to such longings in *Epistle II.ii.*: "The Laws of God, as well as of the Land,/ Abhor, a *Perpetuity* should stand" (252, 247-48). And he replies in a similar way to Swift:

> Well, if the Use be mine, can it concern one
> Whether the Name belong to Pope or Vernon?
> What's *Property?* dear Swift!

(165-67)

But Pope does not stop there. The argument from Use, as though carried by an energy that Swift's extremism had released, widens to become a radical rejection of history itself — which, moreover, is seen to embody a pattern of inevitable decline, not simply a cycle of displacement as in Horace — and an argument for philosophic transcendence of the world:

> What's *Property?* dear Swift! you see it alter
> From you to me, from me to Peter Walter.
>
> .   .   .   .
>
> At best, it falls to some ungracious Son
> Who cries, my father's damn'd, and all's my own.
> Shades, that to Bacon could retreat afford,
> Become the portion of a booby Lord;
> And Hemsley once proud Buckingham's delight,

Slides to a Scriv'ner or a City Knight.
Let Lands and Houses have what Lords they will,
Let Us be fix'd, and our own Masters still.
(167-68, 173-80)

The mixture of loss and gain that had pervaded Pope's image of retirement, the dual attitude with which he had begun the poem, are simplified, in the last lines, to a vision bordering on the otherworldly and an identity both single and self-concentrated. If Swift expresses an intensified version of Bethel's desire for permanence, Pope, at the close, stands at the opposite extreme, articulating a radical version of Bethel's contempt for the world. The image of retirement fades into thin air as the difficulties underlying it are forced into the open through the agency of Swift's criticism.

Satire II.ii. marks that point in the development of the satires at which, as in the epistles, a precarious middling stance crumbles to reveal an underlying dilemma and a lurking need for radical yet impossible choice. Retirement, here as elsewhere, is shown to be a provisional fiction, a false middle term. It is at times a useful fiction, and a necessary one, for much of the poem is a mode of imaginative resistance to the stark dilemma of the end. But the middle way it seems to offer does not really exist. Pope is not merely a maker of fictions by which to live but, necessarily, a critic of them as well. What remains, in the end, is an impossible dilemma and a poet who nevertheless chooses and accepts the loss that his choice imposes.

iv. *The Limits of Resistance:* Epilogue to the Satires

In the *Epilogue to the Satires* (1738), Pope adopts the apocalyptic stance more fully than in any other poem except *The Dunciad.* Yet while the *Epilogue*, like *The Dunciad*, is an extreme case — exacerbating the tensions of earlier poems and uniting the drive toward apocalyptic vision with a powerful effort of resistance to it — it is not a special case. The tensions the poem exacerbates are present throughout Pope's career, as is the apocalyptic vision. Indeed, that vision has a surprisingly insistent place not simply in the poetic life of the poet but in his everyday, or at least his epistolary, life as well. In his letters, Pope's perspective is often genially and self-consciously Olympian. In 1731, for example, he writes that his and Lord Bolingbroke's current works, "with a just neglect of the present age, consult only posterity; and with a noble scorn of politicks, aspire to philosophy."[21] And three years later, after the *Essay on Man* had been published, Pope speaks again from the Olympian perspective. Bolingbroke "is so taken up still (in spite of the monitory Hint given in the first line of my Essay) with particular Men, that he neglects mankind, and is still a creature of this world, not of the universe: this World, which is a name we give to Europe, to England, to Ireland, to London, to Dublin, to the Court, to the Castle, and so diminishing, till it comes to our own affairs, and our own persons."[22] The atmosphere at such heights is heady but thin, and Pope often takes comfort from the more concrete though no less cosmic assurances of physical nature: "I came to Twitnam, where I am in my Garden, amused and easy. This is a Scene where one finds no Disappointments; the Leaves of this year that are fallen, are sure to come on again the next." And the inevitable comparison follows: " 'Tis far otherwise in the Great World, (I mean the Little World) of a Court & c."[23]

At other times, these worlds are not so distinct, and Pope's difficult participation in both is captured in his descriptive imagery. He writes to Swift in 1736:

I see things more in the whole, more consistent, and more clearly deduced from, and related to, each other. But what I gain on the side of philosophy, I lose on the side of

poetry: the flowers are gone, when the fruits begin to
ripen, and the fruits perhaps will never ripen perfectly.
The climate (under our Heaven of a Court) is but cold and
uncertain: the winds rise, and the winter comes on. I find
myself but little disposed to build a new house.... I wish
you had any motive to see this kingdom....I have
indeed room enough, nothing but myself at home! the
kind and hearty house-wife is dead! the agreeable and
instructive neighbour is gone! yet my house is inlarg'd,
and the gardens extend and flourish, as knowing nothing
of the guests they have lost.[24]

The blending of contexts, both figurative and literal, is
remarkable. The garden world, a symbol of cosmic cycle and
continuity at the close, begins as a symbol of Pope's mental
life. When he moves to the "climate" under the courtly
heaven, the metaphor modulates imperceptibly to the
architectural: Pope is no longer producing flowers and fruit,
but considering building a new "house" of poetic and
philosophic materials. And despite the court climate, the
accents of possibility remain: climate becomes mere weather
("the winds rise, and the winter comes on"), and the seasonal
image connects with the more hopeful garden as well as with
the poet's aging and ripening. The passage expresses a
seemingly instinctive resistance to statements of final
hopelessness, a resistance that softens such statements almost
as they are written so that our attention is caught by what is
not certainly hopeless: "I find myself *but little disposed* to
build a new house" (my emphasis).

Three years later, in a letter to Fortescue, Pope speaks of
"the events of a world, I am daily weaning myself away from,
as I think it less and less lovely, and less worthy either
remembrance or concern."[25] "Weaning" is perhaps an odd
word to use of a man who had celebrated his fifty-first
birthday some two months earlier. But it seems appropriate
when we find Pope seven years before this (1732) rejecting
the world in still harsher terms: "The world after all is a
little pitiful thing; not performing any one promise it makes

us, for the future, and every day taking away and annulling the joys of the past."[26] Any effort to discover a linear chronological development of this theme rather than a pattern of recurrence is effectively crushed by a letter from Pope to his young friend George Lyttelton in 1738, the year of the *Epilogue to the Satires*: "I have had but very bad health since you left me, but tis no matter, tis all in the Way to Immortality. However I advise you to live, for the sake of this pretty World, and the Prettiest things in it."[27] Even allowing for the dramatic situation — the aging poet addressing a young member of the Opposition, secretary to the Prince of Wales — one is still impressed by Pope's persistent openness to the world and by his nearly heroic resistance to abjuring it. As he wrote to Swift two months later: "Perhaps, to have a memory that retains the past scenes of our country and forgets the present, is the means to be happier and better contented. But, if the *evil* of *the day* be not intolerable...we *may*, at least we *should*, nay we *must* (whether patiently or impatiently) bear it, and make the best of what we cannot make better, but may make worse."[28] Here, the intensification of resistance is caught in the "postponing" structure of the second sentence: the movement from "*may*" to "*should*" to "*must*," and the series of delays interposed by these — and by the parenthetical phrase — between the perception of our burden and the assumption of it.

When this resistance slackens, in the letters as in the poetry, Pope's perspective becomes genuinely apocalyptic, and his participation in the "actual" world is restricted to warfare against the forces of evil and anguished perception of their might: "I can but Skirmish & maintain a flying Fight with Vice; its Forces augment, & will drive me off the Stage, before I shall see the Effects complete, either of Divine Providence or Vengeance: for sure we can be quite Saved only by the One or punished by the other: The Condition of Morality is so desperate, as to be above all Human Hands."[29]

Or, as he wrote eight years earlier (1730): "I can tell you of no one thing worth reading, or seeing; the whole age seems resolv'd to justify the Dunciad, and it may stand for a public Epitaph or monumental Inscription, like that at Thermopylae, on a *whole people perish'd!*"[30] The world is no longer perceived as a set of particulars, or as a pair of forces at war, but as a totality that is wholly corrupt and wholly "other." Both of these passages locate the final duncification in the future, but it is not a distant future.

The continuing presence of the apocalyptic note in Pope's letters may strike one as extreme or even insincere, particularly when it is combined, as it frequently is, with a certain amount of homely chitchat. But this testifies to the central place of the apocalyptic vision in his thought, early and late, and not to a mere penchant for gestures of foreboding. "I begin," he writes to Steele in 1712, "where most people end, with a full conviction of the emptiness of all sorts of ambition, and the unsatisfactory nature of all human pleasures."[31] The course of experience supplied the apocalyptic consciousness with numerous objects, but the form of its vision, the categories through which it apprehended that experience, did not spring from the world. They were intimately bound up with the identity of the poet—as intimately, in fact, as those counterforces devoted to resisting them.

In the *Epilogue to the Satires*, the two main forms of that resistance are an attention to historical particulars and a persistence in dialogue. The complexity of Pope's tone in the *Imitations of Horace* can help us to notice the remarkable flexibility he displays in the *Epilogue* in responding to the Friend's objections, acting out his suggestions, and attempting — with brilliant irony, to be sure — to achieve a reasonable accommodation. Even more striking than the variety of

Pope's postures is his willingness to adopt them. Martin Price has remarked of the Friend that "one is more impressed by the steady tenor of his resistance [to Pope's satire] than by the specific objections," and something comparable could be said of Pope himself.[32] Pope's willingness simply to listen for so long to an interlocutor who, unlike the Friend in *Satire II.i.,* announces his knavery at the outset, suggests the strength of his concern to find a way of existing honorably in that world to which the Friend's devotion is absolute.

More than any other poem of Pope's, the *Epilogue* catches the pressure of time. It is as though the apocalyptic concern with The End were reflected in the nervous intensity of the present moment; the verse moves forward with all the energy that crackling dialogue can generate. There is occasionally a reflective moment, but we are rarely allowed to forget that Pope is responding, that he is concerned to respond; what he speaks is above all directed. As striking as Pope's impulse to dialogue and relationship, moreover, is his persistence in assimilating an extraordinary range of emotional and intellectual attitudes to the satiric mode. He will not cease to speak and he will speak satirically. His compliance is often mock-compliance, and his elaboration of the Friend's arguments often a withering reduction to absurdity; but the important fact is that these suffice to sustain the dialogue as they sustain the poet's independence. At the conclusion of each dialogue, the relationship breaks down and the poem shifts to a different mode, but up to that point satire and dialogue are inextricably intertwined. Pope's speech in these poems is not simply an expression of distance from the world but also a mode of relationship to it, and the tenuousness of that relationship is the tenuousness of dialogue itself.[33]

We can see this more clearly by considering a related issue. James M. Osborn has remarked that "Pope's chief point in both poems is the dilemma of the satirist, forced to choose between the advantages and disadvantages of writing personal particulars or abstract generalizations."[34] Ever since the dunces began to defend themselves by attacking Pope, this dilemma has been treated as a problem of the satirist's *ethos* or presented character: "Personal satire was lampoon, and the result of spite; general satire was undiscriminating and the result of venomous and impious misanthropy."[35] The dilemma is, however, more usefully seen in terms of the apocalyptic stance and the poet's resistance to that stance. In both dialogues, Pope's discourse with the Friend is sustained until the concluding passages: the Triumph of Vice, and the hymn to ridicule that introduces the vision of the Temple of Eternity. This movement from dialogue to declaration is paralleled by a movement from "personal particulars" to a mode that is not exactly "abstract generalization" but something closer to symbolic vision. The first dialogue provides an example of each:

> Ye Gods! shall *Cibber's* Son, without rebuke
> Swear like a Lord? or a *Rich* out-whore a Duke?
> A Fav'rite's *Porter* with his Master vie,
> Be brib'd as often, and as often lie?
> Shall *Ward* draw Contracts with a Statesman's skill?
> Or *Japhet* pocket, like his Grace, a Will?
> Is it for *Bond* or *Peter* (paltry Things!)
> To pay their Debts or keep their Faith like Kings?
> (I. 115-22)

> *Vice* is undone, if she forgets her Birth,
> And stoops from Angels to the Dregs of Earth:
> But 'tis the *Fall* degrades her to a Whore;
> Let *Greatness* own her, and she's mean no more:
> Her Birth, her Beauty, Crowds and Courts confess,
> Chaste Matrons praise her, and grave Bishops bless:
> In Golden Chains the willing World she draws,
> And hers the Gospel is, and hers the Laws:
> Mounts the Tribunal, lifts her scarlet head,
> And sees pale Virtue carted in her stead!
> (I. 141-50)

The disjunction in modes is emphasized, as Osborn observes, by Pope's annotation: "In Dialogue I the first 134 lines carry twenty-four notes by Pope, an average of one for every six lines. Yet the last thirty-six lines, the passage personifying Vice Triumphant, was left bare of any note from the poet's hand."[36]

These parallel movements — from intense particularity to symbolic vision, and from dialogue to prophetic utterance — mark an access of autonomy in Pope's imaginative perception of society. As the particulars of the poem accrete, they seem to reach a kind of critical mass and reveal a pattern where before there were merely phenomena. History becomes vision. At the same time, the traditional satiric structure dissolves to reveal the unbridgeable gap between the world and the poet, a poet who no longer engages that world, expressing it to itself, but stands back and prophetically passes judgment on it. Seen retrospectively, therefore, the emphasis on historical particulars and the sustaining of dialogue in the first three fourths of the poem signify the reverse of that antisocial name-calling of which the Friend accuses Pope. They express resistance to the isolation of the apocalyptic satirist. Pope does not merely perform a moral duty in attacking particular men and naming names; he also preserves a saving remnant of possibility.

When Pope does abandon the fragments of particularity for the sweeping interpretation of vision, he also abandons the existing community of men, as Lord Bathurst threatened to do in the epistle *To Bathurst:* "You hold the word, from Jove to Momus giv'n,/ That Man was made the standing jest of Heav'n." And as Sir Robert, cynically and hypocritically, has also done:

> Would he oblige me? let me only find,
> He does not think me *what he thinks mankind.*
>   (*Epilogue to the Satires,* I. 33-4, my emphasis)

Unresisted, the apocalyptic vision discerns in random instances of corruption the form of a malign *genius Britannicus* like that envisioned by Lord Bolingbroke in *The Idea of a Patriot King:* "A spirit of slavery will oppose and oppress the spirit of liberty and seem, at least, to be the genius of the nation. Such too it will become in time, when corruption has once grown to this height, unless the progress of it can be interrupted."[37] Here is Pope:

> Lo! at the Wheels of her Triumphal Car,
> Old *England's* Genius, rough with many a Scar,
> Dragg'd in the Dust! his Arms hang idly round,
> His Flag inverted trails along the ground!
> Our Youth, all liv'ry'd o'er with foreign Gold,
> Before her dance; behind her crawl the Old!
> (I, 151-56)

The passage, moreover, records not the temporal movement of history but the working out of demonic principle, as though in an allegorical tableau. Emphasis is thrown onto the moral rather than the kinetic import of the verbs: *dragg'd, hang, trails, dance, crawl.* What is wholly known and wholly corrupt cannot long hold the moral imagination. Pope ends by addressing those uncertain readers of his epitaph for "Old *England's* Genius": "Yet may this Verse (if such a Verse remain)/Show there was one who held it in disdain" (171-72).

Pope's movement from historical satire to apocalyptic vision is a necessary separation from the world of the Friend, but it also liberates a certain visionary momentum. While the beginning of the Triumph of Vice carries on the previous mock-defense of Vice, describing the power that is always Vice's when *"Greatness"* acknowledges her, the Triumph does not remain in this hypothetical mode. With Pope's "Lo!" (151), the ironic and hypothetical becomes the visionary actual until the final couplet, dramatizing that drive toward totality which the apocalyptic impulse seems always to exhibit. "Dialogue II" descends from these heights and partly revives the historical mode; it also opens with an oblique criticism of the visionary flight that closed "Dialogue I." The Friend urges Pope to subordinate historical realities to moral generalization — "Spare then the Person, and expose the Vice" (12) — and Pope's mock-compliance is revealing:

> Come on then Satire! gen'ral, unconfin'd,
> Spread thy broad wing, and sowze on all the Kind.
> Ye Statesmen, Priests, of one Religion all!
> Ye Tradesmen vile, in Army, Court, or Hall!
> Ye Rev'rend Atheists! . . . .
>
> (II. 14-18)

To write satire like this, Pope ironically implies, is to damn not "the Sharper, but the Dice." Yet this is the very mode in which the Triumph of Vice had concluded:

> In Soldier, Churchman, Patriot, Man in Pow'r,
> 'Tis Av'rice all, Ambition is no more!
> See, all our Nobles begging to be Slaves!
> See, all our Fools aspiring to be Knaves!
> The Wit of Cheats, the Courage of a Whore,
> Are what ten thousand envy and adore.
> All, all look up, with reverential Awe,
> On Crimes that scape, or triumph o'er the Law.
>
> (I. 161-68)

Pope's mockery of the Friend's suggestion is also an indirect criticism of his own satiric practice. In the *Epilogue,* as in his correspondence, apocalypse is less a final than a recurrently threatening phenomenon.

The opening of "Dialogue II" turns from apocalyptic vision to revive the historical mode, for there is more, it seems, to be said. In fact, there is too much more: "Vice with such Giant-strides comes on amain,/Invention strives to be before in vain" (6-7). The multiplicity of vicious particulars threatens to weigh down the transforming imagination. This threat can take several forms, and concrete hints of all of them are given in both dialogues. There is the threat of unintelligibility, evoking the complaint of Swift in Pope's time, and in our own that of Reuben Brower, among others: "We do not object that Pope uses contemporary examples, but that he makes so little out of them poetically."[38] Brower cites the following lines, which descend from the visionary to the obscure with surprising rapidity.

> Not so, when diadem'd with Rays divine,
> Touch'd with the Flame that breaks from Virtue's Shrine,
> Her Priestless Muse forbids the God to dye,
> And ope's the Temple of Eternity;
> There other *Trophies* deck the truly Brave,
> Than such as *Anstis* casts into the Grave;
> Far other *Stars* than * and ** wear,
> And may descend to *Mordington* from *Stair.*
>
> (II. 232-39)

Brower might have cited as well this passage from "Dialogue I":

> Come harmless *Characters* that no one hit,
> Come *Henley's* Oratory, *Osborn's* Wit!
> The Honey dropping from *Favonio's* tongue,
> The Flow'rs of *Bubo,* and the Flow of *Y — ng!*
> The gracious Dew of Pulpit Eloquence;
> And all the well-whipt Cream of Courtly Sense,
> That first was *H—vy's, F—'s* next, and then
> The *S—te's,* and then *H—vy's* once agen.
>
> (I. 65-72)

However thoroughly our historical labors permit us to annotate such passages, the verse itself dramatizes one limit that the satirist of particulars must skirt, that of becoming a mere historian of names and things, a maker of lists. This is the case whatever the moral import of those fragments of reality. Homer catalogs ships; Spenser chronicles the kings of Britain; and Whitman lists cities, trades, animals, plants, and parts of the body. But too much of this, as some longish passages in Whitman may suggest, betrays a failure of imagination, a bondage to the reality that ought to be clarified and transformed, rather than suffered in the immediacy of brute fact. There is the related threat of becoming bound to the moment, shackled to time. We see this in the pressure to "print to day" (II. 3), and to look neither forward nor backward (II. 36-37); in Pope's search for the fugitive virtue of the moment (II. 63ff., 95ff.; and with II. 74-76 cf. I. 87-90); and in his candid acknowledgment that the satirist who would also praise must take his virtue when and where he finds it: "*Fr.* They too may be corrupted, you'll allow?/*P.* I only call those Knaves who are so now" (II. 126-27).

If the *Epilogue* shows us the visionary Pope rising to an Olympian view of the spectacle of Vice Triumphant, it also shows us the Pope who resists this exalted perspective, who follows his apocalyptic vision with a second dialogue and a return to history, and who also dramatizes the dangers of such a return, showing that the poet must preserve his imagination from the compulsions of the world while he preserves his soul from its corruptions. Pope reveals the dangers of both extremes, isolation from the world and bondage to it, and he does so in the interest of that doubleness of vision and identity on which his poetry insists. At the close of "Dialogue II," having soared to a vision of the Temple of Eternity and foreseen — if not invoked — his own martyrdom in the cause of Truth and Poetry, Pope allows the Friend the last word:

> *Fr.* Alas! alas! pray end what you began.
> And write next winter more *Essays on Man.*
>> (II. 254-55)

This is a mean-spirited version of that recalling to the world, and to time ("next winter"), which was Arbuthnot's task in

An Epistle to Dr. Arbuthnot. But here there is no synthesis of impulses, no integration of visionary transcendence and worldly participation. At the close of "Dialogue II" the unresolved choice is between absolute transcendence of the world and a bondage to mere cycle, "more *Essays on Man.*" This choice appears throughout Pope's correspondence and informs, in one way or another, all of his major poems of the 1730s. It takes a still more radical form, and reaches its tragicomic conclusion, in the final epilogue that appeared four years after the *Epilogue to the Satires*: Book Four of *The Dunciad.*

5 Pope and Augustan Knowledge

i. *The Structures of Self-Knowledge:* **An Epistle to Dr. Arbuthnot**

IN a reasonably coherent conceptual system like a poet's universe of discourse, it is theoretically possible to approach the center of meaning from any single point. In practice, however, it is better to start at some points than at others; for while each, like a Leibnizian monad, reflects the meaning that informs the whole, some reflect that meaning with great directness and with a minimum of distortion. In Pope's poetic universe, *An Epistle to Dr. Arbuthnot* is such a point, seeming to express the very center of the poet's consciousness and yet moving from that center, as T. R. Edwards puts it, "through all the ranges of tone between cool urbanity and violent moral indignation."[1] *Arbuthnot* is Pope's most ample effort of poetic self-knowledge, his most substantial apprehension of his own nature. The modes of knowledge in which it participates, and the resistance it dramatizes, are part of an act of self-discovery that informs the structural patterns, both large and minute, of the poem.

The underlying pattern of the poem is epistolary: it moves from schematic to substantial knowledge, from retirement to a qualified involvement in the world, and from a dependence on stasis and finality to an acceptance of meaningful process. But *Arbuthnot* differs from the Horatian epistles in several ways, focusing even more than they on the rich and representative complexity of the poet's own life. The epistolary pattern, in this case, becomes a progress from an Augustinian quest for the determining event of the poet's life ("What sin to me unknown/Dipt me in Ink?") to a discovery of the immanent principles controlling the development of that life in time. And while the ending of the poem shares with the other epistles a tentative and provisional attitude, it is nevertheless more securely resolved, more confident that essential contradictions have been harmonized and not merely faced with clarity and candor. Indeed, the very play the poem affords to various extremes seems to make possible a fuller resolution. For *Arbuthnot* punctuates the decorum of the epistle with heroic assertions, intense denunciations, and Olympian pronouncements, incorporating elements of other genres into the epistolary form or extending that form to include them. Of the satires and epistles of the 1730s, *An Epistle to Dr. Arbuthnot* most nearly fuses the two kinds of poem.

These poetic modes, and the aspects of the poet's consciousness they articulate, are fully united in only a few of Pope's poems. *Epistle II.i.* ("To Augustus") offers a limited version of such a union insofar as Pope casts the scornful response of the satirist into the form of the panegyric epistle. But it does so, in part, by shearing away the extremes of both modes and by quite thoroughly subordinating the development characteristic of the epistles to the disclosure that marks the satires. The "eloquent shape" of *Arbuthnot,* as Maynard Mack has said, "comes in large part from the poet's tying his 'Bill of Complaint' against others to a progressive enlargement of vision in himself."[2] In that Bill of Complaint we can discern the pattern of the satires and the thrust toward schematic knowledge. In the progressive enlargement of the poet's vision, we see the pattern of the epistles and the movement toward substantial knowledge. Only *Arbuthnot* offers a fusion of poetic modes, acts of knowledge, and contradictory roles and visions, so various and complete that the poem seems to express, in miniature, the essence of the poet's poetic identity. The central position that *Arbuthnot* occupies in Pope's poetry, moreover, permits us to take the poem as something of an Augustan paradigm, a point from which to plot one significant line of development in eighteenth-century English literature as a whole. That line connects the Augustan attempt to recover the substantiality of experience with the later-eighteenth-century effort to articulate a perception of insubstantiality.[3]

The present opening of *Arbuthnot* was the climax of an early draft of the poem, which began, after six introductory lines, with the autobiographical account that constitutes the second section of the poem as we now know it: "Why did I write? What sin to me unknown/Dipt me in Ink, my Parents', or my own?" (125-26).[4] Pope's restructuring of the poem altered its meaning significantly, in part by making fuller use of the meaningfulness of structure. For one thing, the restructuring provided a better starting point for that enlargement of vision, as Mack puts it, in which the poet moves "from amused self-centered harassment at the opening to outward-looking serenity at the close."[5] For another, it emphasized the poem's structural affinities with the literature of retirement. The poet in this case retreats not only from public confusion to private tranquillity but — within this — from present to past as well. Pope then reconstructs his history as a poet and thus imaginatively "re-lives" his life up to a present that he can now securely inhabit.

The intense inwardness that *Arbuthnot* shares with some of the Horatian epistles is created, in part, by this double retreat but also by its versatile transitions. The most interesting of the transitions are of two extreme kinds, abrupt gaps and imperceptible modulations. In the first case, the impression is one of sudden discontinuity, of a shift of focus that is willed or arbitrary rather than logical or associative (between, for example, lines 26 and 27, 68 and 69, 124 and 125). In the second case, one subject replaces another so gradually or so unapparently that it is difficult simply to locate a transition (for example, 249-64, or 283-304). The introductions to the four major portraits are special instances of these uses of transition. What John Butt calls the "parenthetic position" of the Bufo portrait, for example, results from the fact that Pope first concludes a detailed list of all he has repudiated with the mention of Bufo, but then goes on to describe Bufo. What appeared to be a conclusion, therefore, serves also as an introduction.[6] This portrait falls between the extremes established by those of Sporus and Pope's father, the portrait of the elder Pope growing gently out of the lines that precede it while that of Sporus is imposed by an assertion of will that cannot be contained (Pope catches this brilliantly by "flapping" Sporus in the very process of saying that he wishes to do so). The impression created by transitions such as these is that of a mind thinking and imagining, responding to present associations and thoughts rather than presenting what it has thought at some prior moment. The structure of the verse makes us intensely aware of the medium of consciousness in which the poet reconstructs his past.

One important feature of that medium, in *Arbuthnot*, is its capacity for ambiguity; not merely verbal ambiguity, though there is much of that, but ambiguity of judgment and values. There is the calculated but ultimately self-destructive ambiguity of Atticus, adapted to stylistic ends by Pope in what W. K. Wimsatt has called "the kindly, the pitying and tearful devastation of the 'Atticus' portrait."[7] But there are also minor allusive ambiguities such as the following, to which Pope draws attention in a footnote:

> You think this cruel? take it for a rule,
> No creature smarts so little as a Fool.
> Let Peals of Laughter, *Codrus!* round thee break,
> Thou unconcern'd canst hear the mighty Crack.
> Pit, Box and Gall'ry in convulsions hurl'd,
> Thou stand'st unshook amidst a bursting World.
> (83-88)

Codrus' insensibility takes to ridiculous extremes the just

tenacity of Horace's exemplary figure in Ode III.iii. 7-8.
The effect of the allusion is to keep us aware of the
ambiguity of human qualities, of the way in which a single
trait may prove a virtue or a vice. As Aristotle observes of
disgrace: "He who fears this is good and modest, and he who
does not is shameless. He is, however, by some people called
brave…since the brave man also is a fearless person."[8]
Perhaps the most difficult task Pope sets himself in *Arbuthnot*
is the clarification of his own virtues and impulses in a
context of vices that are closely related to them. The contrast
between the insensible Codrus and Horace's man "just and
tenacious in purpose" is crude, but it is a minor instance in a
process of self-definition surrounded by subtler ambiguities.

The most interesting of these ambiguities concern the poet
directly. On the one hand, he is a nearly helpless victim,
besieged by enemies and importunate flatterers:

> What *Drop* or *Nostrum* can this Plague remove?
> Or which must end me, a Fool's Wrath or Love?
> A dire Dilemma! either way I'm sped,
> If Foes, they write, if Friends, they read me dead.
>   (29-32)

On the other hand, this mad pilgrimage of scribblers to the
poet's home testifies to the immense power that everyone
attributes to him. The poet is both savior and scapegoat, a
literary ruler yet the victim of countless hacks. The same
ambiguity informs the brilliant account of personal flattery
that closes the first section of the poem ("I cough like *Horace*,
and tho' lean, am short" [116]). And it informs the allusions
in the opening lines of the second section: "Why did I write?
what sin to me unknown/Dipt me in Ink, my Parents', or my
own?"[9] Like the biblical allusions, the hint of Achilles is
double edged. Is poetry a mode of strength? Does it also
induce a certain sulkiness, or a pride that can lead one to
forget one's vulnerability? It is not yet possible to say. It is
important, however, to avoid seeing such passages as simply

"mock-anguish" or "tongue-in-cheek,"[10] for the poet is at this point mainly responsive to the negative side of such ambiguities, to his plight as victim. Only in the course of the poem does a mode of self-knowledge emerge that can comprehend, and to some degree resolve, these tensions. Time, therefore, is the crucial dimension of *An Epistle to Dr. Arbuthnot.*

Time enters the poem in two ways. First, it enters in the unfolding of words from beginning to end, and Pope turns this necessary temporality into a specific vehicle of meaning, a dramatization of development. Time also enters by way of the various personal histories that Pope narrates, beginning with the second section of the poem (125). Strictly speaking, the first section is not a history at all since it deals almost exclusively with the typical (the kind of thing that always happens) rather than the historical (what has happened). This shift in mode helps to account for the suddenness of the break between these sections, since the poet moves not only from present to past but also, in Aristotle's terms, from "poetry" to "history."[11] The significance of these modes is that each is the literary form of a mode of knowledge. They dramatize the poet's movement from schematic (or reductive, or apocalyptic) knowledge to that more complex mode, both detached and involved, which may be called substantial or, in the limited sense of the poet's personal history, historical.

The mode of the first section is schematic, and its characteristic action is separation, the disengagement of the satirist from the world that hounds him. The next section (125-72) is a history of engagement, an account of the poet's entrance into society (specifically, literary society), and of his growth from passive precocity — "Well-natur'd *Garth* inflam'd with early praise" — to mature self-assurance: "Did some more sober Critic come abroad?/ If wrong, I smil'd; if right, I kiss'd the rod" (157-58). This history of emergence is followed by a period of equilibrium (173-214) containing the Atticus portrait, which balances Pope against Atticus in a seemingly atemporal moment created by the portrait's "hypothetical" style. The next line begins a history of separation (215). In this history, Pope separates himself not only from "the Race that write," the false patrons, and the world of "Courts" and "great Affairs," but even from the compulsions of the role through which he articulates himself in the world at large, the role of poet. He can sleep without a poem in his head (269), and he begins to feel a minor version of that impingement of role on self which the opening of the poem dramatized:

> Why am I ask'd, what next shall see the light?
> Heav'ns! was I born for nothing but to write?
> Has Life no Joys for me? or (to be grave)
> Have I no Friend to serve, no Soul to save?
>
> (271-74)

At this point, Pope has reenacted the separation of the opening section in substantial and historical rather than typical and schematic terms, understanding it in a more complex and generous fashion; in doing so, he has brought his history up to the present.

This summary has, however, ignored important ambiguities for the sake of clarity. First, Pope's history of engagement is also a history of the attacks he had suffered, and in the retelling there is an increasingly large admixture of satiric retaliation. This grows from the brief gibe at the *"Burnets, Oldmixons,* and *Cooks"* (146), which seems merely tacked on to the poet's account of early patrons and friends, to the full-scale denunciation of "piece-meal critics," which virtually swallows up the autobiographical detail that detonates it (159-72). Pope's history of engagement inevitably and increasingly involves a satiric repudiation, a separation. The converse is also true. Pope's history of separation is increasingly peopled by figures of engagement, of identification and friendship. Dryden, for instance, casually enters the Bufo portrait, not simply as a counterpart to Pope, who also escaped Bufo's "judging eye" (or "judging I"), but also as a link with an earlier passage concerning true friendship and honest patronage:

> But why then publish? *Granville* the polite,
> And knowing *Walsh*, would tell me I could write;
> Well-natur'd *Garth* inflam'd with early praise,
> And *Congreve* lov'd, and *Swift* endur'd my Lays;
> The Courtly *Talbot, Somers, Sheffield* read,
> Ev'n mitred *Rochester* would nod the head,
> And *St. John*'s self (great *Dryden*'s friends before)
> With open arms receiv'd one Poet more.
>
> (135-42)

Similarly, the ironic passage on "the *Great*" following the Bufo portrait modulates imperceptibly into the fine brief elegy on Gay, and the lines on "Prating *Balbus*" obliquely introduce Pope's friendship with Swift, recalling once again the passage just quoted. Precisely at the moment, moreover, in which Pope's detachment is greatest, when he distances himself from even his poetic identity, he turns outward to ask: "Have I no Friend to serve, no Soul to save?" (274).

This intertwining of detachment and engagement occurs so insistently yet so unapparently in the poem as to seem as much a structure of thought as an object, as much a condition of thematic development as a theme. For detachment and engagement describe degrees of involvement in the world, but in a poem like *Arbuthnot* — which re-creates that involvement in the poet's consciousness and discloses its sources there — they also describe modes of consciousness, versions of the satiric and theodicean forms of schematic knowledge. While *Arbuthnot* displays the alternation between these forms of knowledge that appears in some of the other epistles, it nevertheless weds them more thoroughly into the double perspective of substantial knowledge and thus resists the threat posed by either to the life of the spirit.

It is important to distinguish between these threats. We might say that the detachment of satiric schematic knowledge

threatens the life of the spirit *in the world*, and the engagement
of theodicean schematic knowledge threatens the life of the
spirit in the world. The former blinds us to means, the latter
to ends. Thus the end or *telos* of the impulse to engagement
is really a loss of that consciousness of ends which lends
purposiveness to life and makes means simply means. The
reverse is true of the impulse to detachment which, in
spurning means, threatens to deny even their instrumental
necessity. When this "end-consciousness," which is a limited
and personal form of apocalyptic knowledge, overcomes the
genial resistance offered it by the concrete and temporal, by
distraction, by virtually anything — when it overcomes this
to such a degree as to grow absolute — then the world dies to
the spirit. For the aspect of the spirit which is alive to the
world, and which helps constitute the fully human consciousness, has ceased to function.

What form might the poetic expression of such end-
consciousness take? Most obviously, the form of endings.
The numerous abrupt transitions in *Arbuthnot* are of interest
here, for these gaps are ends before they prove also to be
beginnings. Related to these is the curious finality of
portions of Pope's autobiography: the rapid movement from
birth to bodily decay (125-34), the continually revived
beginnings which give the impression that each stage of the
autobiography corresponds not only to a stage in Pope's life
but also to the capacity of the narrating imagination to resist
or postpone a conclusion (an impression that is reinforced
by the increasing length of the stages).

But more significant than these minor forms of ending are
the poem's three major climaxes, the first two of which
correspond to what is called a false cadence in music. The
first major climax concludes the long passage of self-
definition following the Sporus portrait, and ends with the
heroic assertion: "For thee, fair Virtue! welcome ev'n the
last!" (359). The second climax, which was the actual ending
of the poem in the Morgan-Huntington manuscript, con-

cludes the penultimate paragraph: "Oh grant me thus to
live, and thus to die!/ Who sprung from Kings shall know
less joy than I" (404-5).[12] The third climax is the ending of
the poem as we now know it.

A related feature of the poem might seem merely curious
in a work of different concerns: the number of more or less
serious "endings" of Pope himself — deaths, mock-deaths,
final sleeps — that make their way into the verse. There is the
excuse to avoid visitors in the opening couplet ("Say I'm
sick, I'm dead"); the fatal "Dilemma" jokingly entertained in
the address to Arbuthnot (27-32); the vision of a "sleep"
concluding the satiric task (which Pope, erroneously, imagines
here to be less than lifelong [79-82]); Pope's death in the line
of Homer (123-24), and in the line of Gay (261-62). And there
are three other "endings" envisioned more or less explicitly,
and corresponding, moreover, to the three major climaxes
noted above.

The first of the false cadences, which is also a vision of the
poet's end, can serve to illustrate the function of these
numerous endings. It is a superbly climactic and heroic
statement, concluding one of the longest and best known
periods in Pope's poetry (334-59). Declaring himself no slave
to fortune or fame, money or ambition, but a servant of
virtue, and recalling the abuse he has suffered from "the
dull, the proud, the wicked, and the mad," Pope ends with a
ringing reaffirmation of his dedication to virtue: "Welcome
for thee, fair Virtue! all the past:/ For thee, fair Virtue!
welcome ev'n the *last*!" (358-59). What more could there be to
say? The repetition itself suggests that the ultimate statement,
morally and rhetorically, has been made. Yet the interlocutor
immediately questions: " 'But why insult the Poor, affront
the Great?' " Pope answers him ("A Knave's a Knave, to me,
in ev'ry State"), and goes on to give an account of his softer
side: his being "bit" by Sappho, and his charity to Dennis.
From one perspective, this is curiously anticlimactic, a
shocking descent from the dedication to moral heroism that

precedes it. Indeed, considered only in the immediate context, Arbuthnot's question might seem a failure of understanding on his part or a failure of poetic tact on Pope's. Yet it is neither; at least it is surely not the latter. For Arbuthnot does not dilute Pope's virtuous determination; instead, he calls him back from the isolation of the tragic hero, from the absoluteness of the moral vision. Arbuthnot recalls Pope from a concern with last things so intense that it threatens to leave behind the fertile impurity — the substantiality — of things in the world. Indeed, it is not so much what Arbuthnot says as that he says something, that his voice of worldly human concern profanes the high decorum of a premature personal apocalypse.

It is telling, in this connection, that the real ending of the poem shows Pope not recalled but voluntarily turning toward Arbuthnot, toward the world. Pope does not lack hope, nor has he abandoned the moral vision, but he speaks even of death with the accents of life. Here he does not focus exclusively on ends but on extending the process of living as well ("With lenient Arts extend a Mother's breath"), much as Arbuthnot, a friend to Pope's life, has worked to "prolong" that life (27). When Pope at last announces, "Thus far was right, the rest belongs to Heav'n," we may find two meanings in "rest" and take this as the poet's acknowledgment that extreme devotion to purity, exclusive consciousness of ends, may express a longing for rest in this world that cannot be indulged by the moral imagination. Perhaps even "longing" is too psychological a term; it may be more accurate to say that a concern with ends is inevitably a distraction from becoming, and that this concern may threaten to destroy the temporal life of one's consciousness. Thus Arbuthnot, speaking from this world, revives the poet's consciousness of the world, as Pope's "fall" back into history — and into a history of the affections — clearly shows (368-71). In so doing, Arbuthnot serves a choric function much like that described by Northrop Frye:

> A tragic counterpart of the comic refuser of festivity may
> be discerned in a tragic type of plain dealer who may be
> simply the faithful friend of the hero...but is often an
> outspoken critic of the tragic action.... Such a character is
> in the position of refusing, or at any rate resisting, the
> tragic movement toward catastrophe.... The chorus or
> chorus character is, so to speak, the embryonic germ of
> comedy in tragedy.[13]

Arbuthnot, and indeed Pope himself, must resist the
movement toward catastrophe. For the very center of Pope's
identity, unlike that of the tragic hero, is bound up with the
things and the people of this world, and with the sustaining
complexity of that relationship.

Arbuthnot's resistance is prefigured in the rhetorical
structure of the poem's opening section. The mode of this
section, which is typical or schematic, deals in typical
encounters, brief and iconic remarks, rapid characterizations.
These are expressions of the imagination conscious of ends,
the imagination striving to make a point and to reduce
reality to its schemes. Yet these structures are resisted by
something else, something that we can perhaps call "the
imagination content to dwell in means," or the imagination
freed from the pressure of end-consciousness. These terms
are roughly equivalent to the two forms of schematic
knowledge, satiric and theodicean, although a consistently
satiric tone in some portions of the poem may obscure this
distinction. (Within a satiric passage, that is, it may still be
possible to distinguish between the satiric and theodicean
forms of schematic knowledge.) A striking example of this
resistance occurs after Pope administers his punning Horatian
advice, "Keep your Piece nine years":

> Nine years! cries he,
>   who
>   high in *Drury-lane*
>   Lull'd by soft Zephyrs

        thro' the broken Pane,
Rhymes e're he wakes, and
   prints before *Term* ends,
        Oblig'd by hunger and
            Request of friends:
"The Piece you think is incorrect: why take it,
"I'm all submission, what you'd have it, make it."
                                        (41-6)

As this rearrangement shows, the grammatical subordination is intense, and it is made even more so by the accretion of particulars and by the further subordination of "Request of friends," as a joke, to the actual compulsion of hunger. The effect is a powerful deceleration, as though one were walking steadily toward a goal but halving the length of one's steps. The brisk pace is recovered only in the final couplet, which resumes the typical style that the next two-line characterization continues: "Three things another's modest wishes bound,/ My Friendship, and a Prologue, and ten Pound" (47-48).

The same structural pattern appears in the overall development of characterization. At first, the writers besieging Pope are simply a nameless horde, "All *Bedlam*, or *Parnassus*." Then they are partly individualized into such figures as "the Man of Rhyme," the type figures (Cornus) now sharing the stage with realistically named characters (Arthur). These, in turn, are replaced by more detailed descriptions and characterizations, and by extended exchanges between Pope and the would-be writers. (e.g., 55-68). Each new beginning revives the schematic mode, but that mode continually evolves into a more substantial elaboration of the character or situation. This pattern appears at another level in Pope's penchant for inadequate but iconic formulations that are disproved, or at least complicated, by the rest of the poem:

The truth once told, (and wherefore shou'd we lie?)

The Queen of *Midas* slept, and so may I.

(81-82)

The satirist, in these lines, wishes to tell the truth but once and thereby free himself of the messy and unfinal particularity of the world. But truthtelling is a continuous process of naming, explaining, defining, and revealing. Pope's stance displays that will to finality which must be deflected toward the world again, just as the poet's gaze is deflected by Arbuthnot from the heavens of virtuous martyrdom to the friend he is addressing.

After the shutting of the door that begins the poem, Pope's memory and imagination open it just wide enough to establish their less immediate contact with the world. The effect is, perhaps, more than the poet had expected. "To knock at the door of the past," as Henry James discovered, "was in a word to see it open to me quite wide — to see the world within begin to 'compose' with a grace of its own round the primary figure, see it people itself vividly and insistently."[14] At first, in *Arbuthnot*, that world "composes" with the schematic lucidity it always exhibits when we have just rejected it. But it gradually acquires depth and substantiality as more of the poet's consciousness is liberated and begins to resist the drive toward satiric scheme and simplicity. To say, then, that Arbuthnot's function is prefigured in the rhetorical structure of the verse is to say simply that the forces expressed by Arbuthnot are also present — if momentarily latent — in the poet's consciousness. It is partly this ability to express an impulse while resisting it, and to express the resistance as well, that gives the poem much of its depth and leads readers of a biographical persuasion to commend its truth or authenticity. The poem does not merely communicate biographical information, but reveals central forms of the poet's poetic knowledge, his ways of apprehending himself and his world.

Engagement, and the theodicean form of schematic

knowledge, hold a theoretically opposite but practically equivalent threat, atrophy of the individual consciousness. They can lead to a union with the things of this world, an utter absorption in them, that renders one a perfectly adaptable role without a self, like Randall Jarrell's fictional college president who "was so well adjusted to his environment that sometimes you could not tell which was the environment and which was President Robbins."[15] Pope, who does not display much of this, is understandably more willing to risk the imputation of pride than the charge of servility or moral nonentity. Yet his impulse toward accommodation is nevertheless powerful. The whole basis of *Arbuthnot*, its character as an *apologia* — to which Pope calls attention in the Advertisement by acknowledging "the Necessity to say something of *Myself*" — testifies to the strength of this impulse. The poem itself includes Pope's early response to praise (135-44), his writing of conventional descriptive verse, his attentiveness to critics, and the acuteness with which he diagnoses Atticus' fear of independence and the compatibility of that fear with genius (this in a portrait which, for all its destructiveness, identifies the poet quite closely with Atticus). Pope also describes himself as "soft by Nature, more a Dupe than Wit," echoing his own epitaph on Charles, Earl of Dorset, a poem notable for its focus on the conflicting claims of social acceptance and satiric independence, and thus on the importance of reconciling them:

> Yet soft his Nature, tho' severe his Lay,
> His Anger moral, and his Wisdom gay.
> Blest satyrist! who touch'd the Mean so true,
> As show'd, Vice had his Hate and Pity too.
> Blest Courtier! who could King and Country please,
> Yet sacred keep his Friendships, and his Ease.
>
> (5-10)

Pope's kind of engagement is not servility but the capacity to live in the world. Yet to those unable or unwilling to make this distinction, he may seem as much an abject seeker of social acceptance as a nasty punisher of the innocent. This distinction between authentic engagement and utter servility, moreover, is the particular form of a general theme, the contrast between appearance and reality. Throughout his career, Pope displays an almost Spenserian concern with the ambiguity of appearance, with the shell that mimics the outward form of the spirit it lacks. In *The Dunciad Variorum*, for example, Dulness — more like Spenser's Archimago than like a classical deity — feigns "A Poet's form":

> All as a partridge plump, full-fed and fair,
> She form'd this image of well-bodied air,
> With pert flat eyes she window'd well its head,
> A brain of feathers, and a heart of lead,
> And empty words she gave, and sounding strain,
> But senseless, lifeless! Idol void and vain!
> Never was dash'd out, at one lucky hit,
> A Fool, so just a copy of a Wit.
>
> (II. 37-44)

Such mimicry also appears in the fourth book of *The Dunciad* where the "vast involuntary throng" includes, "(last and worst) with all the cant of wit,/ Without the soul, the Muse's Hypocrit" (99-100). And in the prose Advertisement to the satires, Pope again treats the problem of false appearances and the threat they pose to the genuineness they feign:

> And indeed there is not in the world a greater Error, than that which Fools are so apt to fall into, and Knaves with good reason to incourage, the mistaking a *Satyrist* for a *Libeller*; whereas to a *true Satyrist* nothing is so odious as a *Libeller*, for the same reason as to a man *truly Virtuous* nothing is so hateful as a *Hypocrite*.

The "reason" is that the libeler and the hypocrite threaten to taint the very forms through which the satirist and the virtuous man express their moral energy, and thus to obscure the distinction between vice and virtue, false and true, the insensible Codrus and Horace's just and tenacious man.

In *Arbuthnot,* Pope treats the problem of appearances most powerfully in the Sporus portrait, which fuses an overt willfulness ("Yet let me flap this Bug") with an impersonal attack in the name of uprightness and virtue. Maynard Mack has noticed the crucial dramatic function of the portrait: "Something pretty close to the intensity exhibited by this portrait was called for, at this point...by the drama of feelings that has been building inside the poem — the fictive war — 'the strong Antipathy of Good to Bad,' here projected in its climactic symbol."[16] Although the Sporus portrait is a major battle in the fictive war it is also a curiously personal one; its sources lie in the whole complex of feelings originating in the impulse to engagement. Sporus displays, as G. Wilson Knight puts it, "an utter lack of self-realization, of psychic wholeness," but what above all provoke the poet's wrath are the tinsel glitter, the specious attractiveness, and the chameleon-like adaptability that proceed from this lack of wholeness.[17] Sporus is "one vile Antithesis," his wit "all seesaw between *that* and *this*." He is an "amphibious Thing," capable of "acting either part." As with Satan, however, there are those who attend to him and find him plausible, and who fail to distinguish between his mere adroit indefiniteness — which lacks a center — and the flexibility of a true self. Those who do so, moreover, will confuse a Sporus with a Pope by equating certain undeniable but superficial resemblances; this is the source of the intensity of Pope's tone. In attacking Sporus, Pope attacks the negation that his own difficult flexibility might seem to be, if imperfectly understood, or might threaten to become, if not resisted. The intensity of the attack is the intensity aroused by a debased but skillful parody of oneself.[18]

Pope displays the flexibility of true character in this

poem. If Sporus is cast in the role of Satan, a benign Proteus could well be the most apt emblem for Pope in *An Epistle to Dr. Arbuthnot*. Pope hints at this in the image of himself "seiz'd and ty'd down to judge," and there is perhaps an oblique reflection of Proteus' ability to see "What is, what was, and is to come" in the poem's temporal structure.[19] More significantly, some of the most intense lines in the Sporus portrait (323-25) recall a passage in Waller's "Upon Ben Jonson" that explicitly praises Jonson for the Protean richness of his character and art:

> The sundry postures of thy copious Muse
> Who would express, a thousand tongues must use;
> Whose fate's no less peculiar than thy art;
> For as thou couldst all characters impart,
> So none could render thine, which still escapes,
> Like Proteus, in variety of shapes;
> Who was nor this, nor that, but all we find,
> And all we can imagine, in mankind.
>
> (25-32)

Such echoes and allusions are given point by the poet's ability to inhabit an ambiguous world, to adapt to its conflicting claims, while never surrendering his independence or forgetting that this world and his place in it are inescapably problematic. It is Pope's resistance to simple extremes, his tenacious and imaginative denial of the exclusiveness of mutually exclusive ends, that creates the central man inhabiting the Protean flux.

The Sporus portrait also climaxes the series of definitions of satire that the poem has been implicitly developing, and which parallels the poet's movement from schematic to substantial knowledge. In the first section (1-124), satire is personal self-defense, a way to keep people from bothering you. Satire is not seen as a moral or social force; indeed, its social efficacy is severely questioned (83-108). Satire is next seen as impartial judgment, a naming of "true merit" (175)

that serves truth and not simply the poet. In the portrait of
the Fop (283-304), these definitions gradually fuse. Satire is
here seen as a moral judgment of bad men, but it is also self-
defense. It expresses "the strong Antipathy of Good to Bad,"
but it is also deeply rooted in that need to repudiate that
constitutes part of the poet's act of self-definition. Thus
Pope's deepest argument in this most inward of "program
satires" is twofold. First, he shows that satire is not something
external to the self but an expression of that self toward the
world in which it is located, and thus a vital act of discovery
and self-discovery. Second, he demonstrates and recovers
the continuity of that self, the persistence through its
Protean metamorphoses of an identity that must be metamorphic to be authentic. The discovering consciousness,
moreover, makes part of that metamorphic identity. Its
operation is much like that of Enlightenment reason as Ernst
Cassirer has described it: "Reason does not exclude motion;
it seeks rather to understand the immanent law of motion. It
is reason itself that now plunges into the stream of becoming,
not in order to be seized and carried along by its swirls but in
order to find here its own security and to assert its stability
and constancy."[20]

The true form of Pope's dynamic identity is defined
implicitly and negatively at three points in *Arbuthnot*. First,
Pope's heroic welcome of "the *last*" (359) illustrates the
dangers of courting the absolute, of a too intense desire for
existence out of time. Second, Sporus illustrates the reverse:
an utterly unprincipled descent into becoming. But Atticus
illustrates the dangers of attempting to avoid rather than
incorporate these extremes. In shrinking from the risks of
both isolation and engagement, in trying to create a state
that is free from extremes rather than a dialectical process
participating in them, Atticus inevitably joins Prior's Jack
and Joan in leading not a life but "a kind of — as it were."[21]
Pope's final triumph in *An Epistle to Dr. Arbuthnot* is to show
us the creativeness of his act of self-knowledge by directing

his resistance to the fashioning of a difficult but stable and positive identity. "For what to shun will no great knowledge need,/ But what to follow, is a task indeed" (*To Bathurst,* 201-2).

An Epistle to Dr. Arbuthnot includes aspects of both the epistles and the satires and to a great degree holds together their extremes. The self-examination of the poem is largely an examination of the past, and this helps to mute the immediacy and pressure characteristic of that examination in the epistles. The same may be said of the satiric element insofar as Pope defines himself in contrast to figures whom he re-creates in memory and not those he encounters in dialogue. For the same reason, the distinction between development and disclosure as modes of self-presentation is not altogether sharp. Pope's past character is disclosed, but the effort of self-knowledge that discloses it also discovers its continuity with the poet's present self and thus constitutes a genuine development. We get some idea of the special place of this poem in the poetry of the 1730s when we realize that Arbuthnot, in one sense the typical friend and audience of the epistles, is also a benign version of the timid and worldly adversary of the satiric dialogues, the "Friend" who strives to recall Pope from heroic virtue to the meaner concerns of political prudence and personal safety.[22]

The ending of *Arbuthnot,* like that of the other epistles, is tentative rather than final, but its tentativeness is a mature recognition of the fundamental precariousness of experience. Self-examination will at some future time be required; moral choices will arise and demand to be met; friends, parents, and the poet himself will die. There is no final rest or resolution within this life. But by this recognition, more than in the other epistles, Pope frees himself from the local, the idiosyncratic, the merely personal, and faces the future